Getting
to Know the
PROPHETS

Again for the First Time

RICHARD C. KELLEY AND LEO F. PETERSON

authorHOUSE®

AuthorHouse™
1663 Liberty Drive
Bloomington, IN 47403
www.authorhouse.com
Phone: 1 (800) 839-8640

Published by AuthorHouse 01/18/2018

ISBN: 978-1-5462-2351-1 (sc)
ISBN: 978-1-5462-2350-4 (e)

Library of Congress Control Number: 2018900099

Print information available on the last page.

PART ONE

Dedication: To my children and grand children
Contributing Editors: Richard C. Kelley
                    Leo F. Peterson
Graphic Art: Sharon Vaupel
Proof Readers: Kris Rehfeld and Nancy Davis

The Table of Contents

1. Jonah ....786 – 746 1

2. Amos ....783 – 745 7

3. Hosea..............750 – 725 18

4. Isaiah ....800 – 700 32

5. Micah ....750 – 687 47

6. Nahum...........700 – 612 56

7. Zephaniah.....640 - 625 64

8. Jeremiah ....628 – 586 71

SETTING THE STAGE FOR THE PROPHETS

The high point of Jewish history, in the eyes of some scholars, were the years of King David and King Solomon and their forty-year reigns, from 1010 B.C. to 930 B.C. Following the death of Solomon, the kingdom split into two kingdoms. There was a northern kingdom which was called Israel and a southern kingdom which was called Judah. Judah was made up of the tribe of Judah and the remnants of Simeon. Judah included the city of Jerusalem in its territory, along with the Ark of the Covenant. The kingdom of Israel was made up of ten of the original twelve tribes of Israel. The king of the northern kingdom in 922 B.C. was Jeroboam. He moved quickly to create an identity for Israel. He named two shrine cities, Dan and Bethel, to replace the attraction of going to Jerusalem. He built two golden calves, one for each shrine city, as a symbol to counteract the Ark of the Covenant and the temple of Jerusalem. It is to be noted that Israel would only be given the promised land to possess if it remained faithful to God's Covenant. The stage is now set for the writing prophets to make their appearance in Jewish history. When the people refused to listen to the voice of the prophets, God was forced to act to let the people and the leaders know that He was in charge of salvation history. He dealt first with the northern kingdom and later with the southern kingdom. The capital city of Samaria was destroyed in 722 B.C. and Jerusalem was destroyed in 587 B.C. The title prophet indicated that the person did not speak their own words, but the words of God. Failure to listen and obey God's words will lead to dire consequences. It was the prophet's responsibility to relate God's message to the leaders, priests, prophets and people, regardless of whether or not they are inclined to listen and obey.

A Study of the Prophet

An Introduction

Is it possible that a study of the prophets will be able to teach us anything about what is happening in today's world? The answer is a resounding "yes!" There are four major prophets and twelve minor prophets. Should it happen that any of them by chance would be discovered walking our streets today, they would not be found to be out of place. Their collective messages are as valid today as when they were first uttered over three thousand years ago. They are the epitomization of "those who do not know or respect history are in grave danger of repeating it." Salvation history is the gradual unfolding of God's plan for all human beings. God desires that all people be saved. Everyone will be given the opportunity to experience Jesus face to face before death. The message of the prophets is quite clear. God is kind and merciful, willing to forgive all who repent. What does it take to become a prophet? It takes a personal encounter with God. It takes a commission, an endowment with a mission, a directive by God to tell people what they need to hear. Many prophets believed in what they had been asked to do. Some were poets, statesmen, social critics, moralists and commentators on the human condition. Many felt that it was their responsibility to proclaim the word of God as it had been revealed to them. There are examples today of reluctant missionaries. A priest friend of mine recently celebrated his fortieth year of service to the Lord in California. As a member of a priestly order he was assigned to work in America. His vow of obedience encouraged him to accept each new assignment with graciousness and compliance. He noted that with every new assignment, he experienced a reluctance to embrace with enthusiasm what he had been asked to do. Eventually, in every case he had to admit that his superiors had been correct in their assignment. After eight years in my parish he was asked to go to a foreign country. Less reluctant then Jonah, he accepted his assignment with graciousness and enthusiasm. Jonah is a prime example of reluctant obedience. When he was asked to go to Nineveh, a people he hated, he tried to run away. Those who are familiar with the Book of Jonah know the rest of the story. Nineveh was a large, corrupt city, full of wickedness, with over one hundred and twenty thousand residents. Jonah was to ask them to repent of their sins and God in his graciousness was willing to forgive them. They responded to Jonah's message in a positive manner. God saw the change and did not carry out His threat of destruction of their city. Jonah was unhappy. Jonah's example set the stage for the rest of the prophets, regardless of one's personal feelings, regardless of one's personal inclinations, obedience to God is the most precious commodity prophets possess. They are responsible for delivering God's message to the people in need of that information. The prophets spoke to Judah, to Israel, and to foreign nations as part of God's plan for salvation. People needed to hear the truth. It may not be popular, it may not be fashionable, it may not be easy to accept, but it must be expressed. The more things appear to change the more they stay the same. People are being beheaded in the twenty-first century just as they were at the time of John the Baptist. The tomb of Jonah was destroyed in 2014, his message of repentance, rejected in favor of violence. Clearly the prophets are as relevant today, their message as real as when it was first delivered. For this reason alone, a looking into of the prophets is necessary, important and worthwhile.

The Nature of Prophecy

Most religions, if not all, have produced the phenomenon of prophecy. A prophet is one who speaks for another. The means of prophetic communication were, in general, the same that are presupposed in OT prophecy: dreams, visions, ecstatic or mystical experiences and various divinatory practices. There is no reason to restrict the prophetic spirit of God exclusively to Jewish or Catholic traditions. Although the church has never officially applied the term "prophet" to anyone not so named in Scripture, it is clear that God spoke to his people through such instruments as Francis of Assisi, Catherine of Siena, Saint John of the Cross and others. The word "oracle" means the revelation of a prophet, revealing to people what God has spoken. Classical prophets still use the term "spirit of God" to describe their source of prophetic messages. That being said individuals were not inclined to line up with their application to apply for the job of becoming a prophet. Prophets were not particularly popular, they were often misunderstood, criticized, ridiculed, persecuted, and in some cases martyred. Their life expectancy was not that great. We will begin our look into the prophets with Jonah. People more astute than I recognize just how little agreement exists regarding the key issues of authorship, style and ownership of the books and their component parts.

CHAPTER ONE

The Prophet
Jonah

Richard C. Kelley and Leo F. Peterson

Jonah

Jonah was a prophet who lived during the reign of king, Jeroboam II (783 – 743 B.C.). He is mentioned in the book of 2 Kings, chapter14:25, as a prophet who predicts that king Jeroboam II will be able to expand his kingdom to reestablish the ancient frontiers and borders of Israel. The book was compiled in the fifth century. It is the story of a reluctant prophet who attempted to run away from his divine mission. He boarded a ship headed away from Nineveh. God sent a storm, which resulted in Jonah being cast overboard to save the sailors on board the ship. He was swallowed by a great fish and ultimately, he was deposited on the shore where he was to carry out his mission. Jonah became angry, when the Ninevehites received God's message and repented. The book ends with the story of the gourd plant. The book emphasizes the possibility and desirability of repentance, as well as the merciful and forgiving nature of God. Jonah is selfish in bemoaning his personal loss of a shady gourd plant, without any apparent concern over the loss of life of the inhabitants of Nineveh. This book is the story of a disobedient, narrow-minded prophet, who fails to appreciate God's love and mercy for all who repent of their sins. In the end, Jonah does the right thing. The book of Jonah establishes the sovereignty of God. All nations are to be held accountable for their actions as the other prophets will make perfectly clear in our on-going discussion of the remaining fifteen prophets. Jonah was asked to preach God's word, against the wicked behavior of the Ninevehites. The book presents the universal love of

God, even for the Gentiles. It ridicules some of the narrow nationalistic view held in Judah. It affirms that God is "just" in his actions. God is sovereign and cannot be controlled. God's plan of salvation embraces everyone. The legendary city of Nineveh represents all that is hateful, repugnant, and cruel in an oppressor. Jonah is told to call Nineveh to repentance. They will have forty days to repent. Jonah takes residence outside the city in the hope that God will destroy the city. When Jew or Gentile repent of their sins God is disposed to show mercy and love. The nature of God's message is a change from judgment and punishment, to a call to repentance. Jonah desires to see Nineveh destroyed and is angry when it does not happen. The reality of God's mercy bestowed on a people who, by any definition of justice, seem totally unworthy of such mercy. Jonah's mission is to proclaim the word of God to the entire world. We are all to be held accountable for our actions. Faith is to be shared. We are to love one another as we make our journey through life. Know that the Lord is with you! Today's world seeks love, peace and understanding which begins with the individual.

Reflections and Comments

The law of unintended consequences:

We read in the Book of Kings how Jonah predicts that the king of Israel will restore the boundaries of Israel. This simple statement will lead to an alliance with the king of Syria who in turn will convince Israel that to attack Judah is a good thing. Judah will enter into an alliance with Assyria seeking their protection and inviting them into the area, which will lead to the destruction of Samaria in 722. What was seen as a good thing, the expansion of territory, ends in the destruction of the capital city of Israel. Without the expansion, there would likely not have been an alliance with Syria and no discussion of an attack on Judah.

The Lord is kind and merciful:

There are no limits to the kindness and mercifulness that God is willing to extend to sinners. Not only is God sovereign but forgiveness is to be found with all who are willing to repent of their sins. Nineveh was the capital city of the Assyrian empire. They were a cruel and atrocious enemy of the Israelites and yet God was willing to forgive their offenses if they repent. God extends His hand to all humans. God's grace is offered to all.

Do on to others:

Jonah discovered that resistance to God's call works out in the end. God has a plan of salvation for all. His plans will never be frustrated. They may experience delay but God's grace is available to everyone and it will come to pass. Whether we take advantage of that opportunity for grace is our choice. The door to God's grace opens from the inside.

Jonah

Chapter 1   **The Disobedient Prophet**

1:1 – 2   Jonah's call to mission

1:3   A flee to Tarshish

1:4 – 6   A violent storm

1:7   Casting lots

1:8 – 9   I am a Hebrew

1:10 – 12   Calming the sea

Chapter 2   **A Prayer of Thanksgiving**

2:1 – 2   The Lord sends a big fish

2:3 – 10   A psalm to the Lord

2:11   Jonah set a shore

Chapter 3   **Jonah's Mission accomplished**

3:1 – 5   Nineveh repents

3:6 – 10   The Lord is kind and merciful

Chapter 4   **Anger and Reproof**

4:1 – 4   Jonah is upset

4:5   Jonah leaves Nineveh

4:6 – 7   A gourd plant

4:8	Jonah baked in the sun
4:9 – 10	A conversation with God
4:11	God shows his concern for the inhabitants of Nineveh

The New American Bible: pages 1007-1009
Copyright: Catholic Publishers, Inc. 1971
A Division of Thomas Nelson, Inc.

CHAPTER TWO

The Prophet
Amos

Amos

Amos was a sheepherder and a grower of sycamore figs. He was not a "professional" prophet. He had not spent most of his life pursuing the life of a prophet. Prophets were a common phenomenon in the Middle East. There were court prophets, administrative prophets, and those who earned their living as professional prophets. Amos had been instructed by God to go to the city of Bethel to preach a message of judgment, a message of accountability, a message of destruction and retribution for sins committed. Moses had warned the people that their welfare and survival was linked to their moral behavior. Amos would remind the people that they had turned away from the service of their God, pointing out that they had failed to live up to their commitment to walk with their God in their mutual covenant relationship. They were not behaving as true Israelites. In his farewell desert speech, Moses had warned the people not to be influenced by their neighbor's behavior, they were expected to remain faithful to their God. Amos was from a small town ten miles south of Jerusalem and six miles south of Bethlehem. He was not familiar with an affluent society. He was a farmer and not a city-slicker. He was able to see the disparity that existed between the rich and the poor that marked the Israelite society. In addition to his message of judgment, he was able to speak of God's mercy and forgiveness should the people and their leaders return to the service of the Lord. When Amos spoke against foreign nations, Israel was pleased to hear that God was disappointed with their neighbors. On the other hand, they did not appreciate having the finger of God's judgment being pointed squarely at them. The kingdom of Israel was under indictment. They had failed to live up to the conditions of the covenant relationship established by Moses, accepted by God and to be lived in the lives of God's chosen people. Among the many disappointments listed by Amos, first and foremost, was their treatment of the poor, the orphan, the foreignor and the widow. God was not pleased with their flagrant disregard for God's rules regarding "pledge garments," the taking of bribes, the oppressing of the just and their callous disregard and insensitivity for the plight of others. God did not appreciate their shallow festivals, their noisy songs, their lack of respect, their complacent attitude and their self-indulgent ego-centered self-satisfaction. Israel was experiencing a period of unprecedented wealth and prosperity. They had fallen away from their commitment to live the Ten Commandments and they had gotten away from living their covenant relationship. The "classical" prophets are those found in the Old Testament. Their teachings have been preserved and their names appear at the head of the prophetic books. All of the "classical" prophets received their call from God and that call is referenced in their works. Everyone in Israel knew that false prophets did exist. That is not to say that false prophets deliberately sought to deceive their benefactors. Often the prophets told the king and his advisors what they wanted hear. Certainly it was in their own best self-interest to keep their employers happy. Some of those, who were considered to be false prophets were sincere, but misguided, erring in judgment, confusing their own hopes and desires with the word of God. The "classic" prophets are those who have stood the test of time and are found in the Old Testament. 1 Kings 22:6 gives us an example of 400 court and administrative prophets advising the king of Israel and the king of Judah to take a given course of action, not advise by Micaiah, a prophet of the Lord, who had consulted the Lord in this matter. The king of Israel had Micaiah arrested because he had refused to tell the king what he wanted to hear. The king died in battle, failing to heed what God's prophet had foretold would happen. The role of the prophet was to reveal the mind of God to his chosen people. The tragedy of Israel and Judah was their failure to listen to the prophets sent by God to guide them on their life journey. The prophet Amos told the people and their leaders that unless they changed their ways, their leaders would be killed and the people taken into exile. Prophets tend to tell very little about themselves. Amos was no exception. He was not a professional prophet. He lived in the south and God asked him to go to the north, to the shrine of Bethel. When he proclaimed his message, the local prophets asked Amos to leave the area as he was costing them revenue. They wanted Amos to leave the area, to go home and stop bothering them. The earliest of the writer prophets, he was active at the beginning of the eighth century (783-743). He came from a small village named Tekoa in Judah. The Lord brought me from behind the flock and said to me, "Go! Prophesy to my people in Israel." (Amos 7:14 – 15). Amos then delivers the strong words of the Lord's judgment leveled against both the king and the people of northern Israel. Amos sees injustice all around him, a society bent on wealth and prosperity, a people who had forgotten the true worship of God. "You sell the just person for silver; and the poor for a pair of sandals" (Amos 2:6). You oppress the poor, crush the needy, you use false weights to cheat people. You ignore the words of God at your own peril." He calls the people back to the high moral standards and religious behavior demanded by entering into a relationship with God. His is a powerful voice, which challenges Israel's hypocrisy and injustice. He boldly indicts kings, priests, and leaders. Israel was experiencing a period of wealth and prosperity. The rich were getting richer and the poor were being neglected. Not unlike today! Amos' basic message stresses God's power and supreme sovereignty over the entire world. God holds Israel particularly responsible to live a just and upright way of life. God has concern for the outcast, the oppressed, and the poor. God tells Israel, "Therefore I punish you for all your iniquities." (Amos 3:2) "You shall lose your land; be sent into exile and your leaders shall all be killed." (Amos 6:7-9) Israel has forgotten the true worship of God; they have turned their attention to acquiring wealth and prosperity. They have turned their backs on the Ten Commandments and violated the Covenant of Mount Sinai. There are consequences to be visited upon Israel's behavior. If the people do not change their ways, they will be punished. The people of Israel cannot be God's people unless they live morally upright lives, obey the commandments, and respect the Laws of Moses. The Book of Amos moves from a condemnation of the evil found in other nations, to the terrible injustice and evil present in Israel, to the visions of Divine punishment that is coming upon the people and their leaders. Israel had fallen into idol worship; they had become callous, indifferent and filled with hypocrisy regarding social justice and the care of the poor. Forgetful of the true worship of God, they engaged in carless religious ritualism. "Take away from me your noisy songs." (Amos 5:23).

Reflections and Comments

The More things change:

While Jonah is known as the reluctant prophet, Amos on the other hand, accepted his calling without whining, complaining, or even doubting that God had commissioned him to preach to the northern kingdom. The message Amos delivered was truthful, strong, and unyielding. Amos knew that God's words had to be expressed, even if their reception, from a gatherer of figs and a herder of sheep, would not be appreciated, listened to, or even followed. He was appaled by the lack of concern for the widow, the foreignor, and the poor. He decried the "I've got mine" attitude displayed by the rich. Israelites welcomed Amos' words, when he spoke about the crimes of their neighbors. They took exception when he addressed Israel and Judah for the crimes that they were guilty of and for their departure from the conditions and terms of God's Covenant. A reoccurring theme expressed by Amos was God's plea to return to the service of the Lord. God is asking them to stop and consider what it is that they are doing. God tells them that He has grown tired of their lip service. "I take no pleasure in your solemnities." Their hearts are caught up in worldly concerns. The same observation could easily be made about today's society. We appear to be worried about, "What's in it for me?" or "When do I receive my share?" Pope Francis has drawn attention to the needs of the poor and to our responsibility to return to the service of our God. His message is exactly the same message that Amos gave to the Israelities three thousand years ago.

Do the right thing:

Amos issued to Israel and to Judah a **call** to change their behavior, a **call** to stand up for what is right, not what is popular, a **call** to do the right thing, not what is self-serving. They must learn to thank God for blessings received and be willing to share with others what is not required. "What will I return to the Lord, for all that He has done for me?" Amos asked the people and their leaders to "Return to the service of the Lord." Amos' message has stood the test of time; it is as relevant and as important to us, today, as it was to Israel and Judah in their day. The words that Amos spoke became reality around fifty years later. Death and destruction lie in their future. All they had to do was honor the warning of Moses. "Do not get caught up in the ways of the world!" Famine, fire, crumbling walls, were part of the visions Amos received. All the Israelites had to do was the right thing.

History has a habit of repeating itself:

God's chosen people, the Israelites had to face the trials and tribulations posed by Assyria, Babylon, Persia, Greece, and the Romans in Old Testament times. Today they face Hamas, Hezbollah, ISIS, a number of extreme Islamic groups, and anyone dedicated to the total destruction of Israel.

An Epilogue:

Amos offers hope to those who choose to listen to the words of the Lord. Yes, there will be tough times, times of suffering, times of great pain, times that the nation could have avoided had they been willing to listen, to change, to live as the Lord had asked them to live. Amos' message is timeless; it is meant for all ages. "Return to the Lord!" The same is true today. We have drifted away for the service of the Lord. We have gotten caught up in the things of the world. A look at the words of Amos in the scriptures will remind us. "Return to the Lord"

Amos

Chapter 1   **A Breeder of Sheep from Tekoa**

1:1 – 2   Commissioned by the Lord
1:3   A list of offenses against the Nations
1:3 – 5   For three crimes of Damascus
1:6 – 8   Philistia's offenses
1:9 – 10   Tyre
1:11 – 12   Edom
1:13 – 15   The Ammonites

Chapter 2   **The List Continues**

2:1 – 3   Moab
2:4 – 5   Judah
2:6 – 16   The list of Israel's crimes

Chapter 3   **Hear the Words of the Lord**

3:1 – 2   I will punish all your iniquities
3:3 – 6   Answer these questions
3:7   The Lord's plan revealed
3:8 – 15   Israel must pay for crimes committed

Chapter 4   **Woman of Samaria**

4:1 – 3   You who oppress the destitute

4:4 – 6   You did not return to the Lord

4:7 – 9   You did not heed the signs

4:10 – 13   Return to the Lord: Now!

Chapter 5   Hear the Words of the Lord

5:1 – 3   A Word of Lament

5:4 – 9   Amos asks Israel to Repent

5:10 – 17   There will be a Day of Reckoning

5:18 – 27   A Day of Punishment is to Come

Chapter 6   Woe to the Complacent

6:1 – 3   A Word to the Overconfident

6:4 – 7   The Wealthy be Warned

6:8 – 11   Only a Few will Survive

6:12 – 14   The Lord has had Enough

Chapter 7   Symbolic Visions

7:1 – 3   First Vision: The Locust Swarm

7:4 – 6   Second Vision: The Rain of Fire

7:7 – 9   Third Vision: The Plummet

7:10 – 14   Amaziah tells Amos "Leave"

7:15 – 17   Amos' response to Amaziah

Chapter 8   **The Visions Continue**

8:1 – 3   Fourth Vision: The Summer Fruit
8:4 – 8   Stop Exploiting My People
8:8 – 14   A Day of Judgment is Coming

Chapter 9   **The Destruction of the Sanctuary**

9:1 – 10   Fifth Vision: The Altar
9:11 – 15   The Epilogue: Hope in the Future

The New American Bible: pages 996-1006
Copyright: Catholic Publishers, Inc. 1971
A Division of Thomas Nelson, Inc.

CHAPTER THREE

The Prophet
Hosea

Hosea

Our third prophet is Hosea. As with the other prophets, we know very little about him. From his writings, we know that he had a difficult personal life. He experienced firsthand what God experienced when dealing with the people of Israel. The lies, the deceit, the fickle attitude, the moral corruption, the lack of commitment associated with one who has lost their way, all these were part of the overall picture which God and the prophet had to contend with in their attempts to rekindle the fire of God's love and rescue Israel from their reckless unfaithfulness. Israel's prosperity ended when the king of Israel, Jeroboam II died in 746 B.C. His son ruled for six months before he was murdered. His murderer ruled for only one month before he was killed. Political intrigue, conspiracy, assassinations and instability marked the kingdom right up to its destruction in 722 B.C. Hosea was a contemporary of Jonah and Amos and in later years with Isaiah and Micah. Prophets were a common aspect of life in the Middle East. Hosea had grown up in the northern kingdom of Israel and as such he was familiar with all the things Amos had chronicled in his indictment of the leaders of Israel. He knew how the poor were treated, how poor farmers lost their land and were sold into slavery, how the money changers had rigged the system to favor the rich, even how the people gave lip service to their worship while their hearts were far from the God of Israel. Hosea like Amos reminded the people that in their turning away from the service of God there was clear evidence of their failure to live up to their commitment to walk with their God in their mutually agreed covenant relationship. Moses had told the people not to be influenced by their neighbor's behavior. They were expected to remain faithful to the tenants of their faith and the conditions of their covenant relationship. They were to live in the world without becoming a part of the world. Hosea had harsh words for the self-seeking and irresponsible kings and leaders. Hosea knew that the political upheaval was symptomatic of much deeper problems. Israel had forsaken God and turned to the worship of the fertility gods of Canaan, the Baals. Hosea condemned the overt and open practice of paying homage to the Baals, false gods. He condemned the merging of the cult of Baalism with the worship of the God of Israel, the intermixing of rites. The God of Israel was held in the same esteem as the pagan gods. Understandably, he compared what the Israelites were doing to harlotry. Hosea was deeply troubled with the behavior of the Israelites. Israel had forsaken its true lover Yahweh and had given itself over to the service of pagan gods. Israel was guilty of spiritual apostasy. Hosea knew that Israel was in trouble and that they were headed for destruction. Assyria had managed to gain a foothold in the area having been invited in by the king of Judah. Jonah had prophesied in 2 Kings 14:25 that the expansion of Israel would take place. The result of this expansion ended in an alliance with Damascus, which in turn evolved into a later threatened war with Judah. Judah, seeking protection from Damascus and Israel, turned to Assyria for help. The king of Judah, Ahaz, was told by the prophet Isaiah not to enter into any foreign alliance. Ahaz failed to listen to Isaiah and asked Assyria for help, and as they say, "the rest is history." Hosea knew it was a matter of time before Samaria would be destroyed by Assyria. As Amos had done, so Hosea, in a similar fashion, expressed God's message of judgment. Both prophets spoke about God's mercy and forgiveness, hoping that the people and their leaders would come to their senses and return to the service of the Lord. Hosea was more optimistic than Amos regarding the possibility of Israel's return to the Lord. Among the many frustrations and disappointments, the prophets experienced, there was Israel's callous disregard and insensitivity for the plight of the poor and others. Sin brings with it consequences that reach beyond one's immediate concerns. As we shall see, Israel's infidelity and disrespect for God will lead to the ultimate destruction of Samaria and to an end of Israel's influence in the region. Hosea was a man who had deep feeling for his people. He knew that is was during this chaotic period of political intrigue that they had strayed from the service of the Lord. He had been born, educated, and raised in the north and he knew that the people were better than they were behaving. They needed to be reminded just how great their God was, just how much God loved them and how special their relationship. He worked from about 745 B.C. down to at least 722 B.C. and perhaps longer. It seems that he experienced a very painful marriage in which his wife proved unfaithful on more than one occasion. In his book, Hosea describes his own life, surrounded by moral corruption, even an unfaithful wife, painting a picture that parallels the unfaithfulness and breaking of the bond of love between God and Israel. His book demonstrates just how seriously sin affects a covenant relationship between a man and a woman and a nation and their God. Hosea, Isaiah, Jeremiah, and Ezekiel all used the image of marriage and the unfaithfulness found therein to describe Israel's and Judah's unfaithfulness in their dealings and their relationship with their God. God's generous and even passionate love for his people is met with ingratitude, disdain, and indifference. In Israel's case their religious infidelity took the form of worshipping false gods, ignoring the Ten Commandments, and disrespecting the Covenant. Hosea preached a message of punishment and judgment that was certain to come. He listed the violations against justice, the oppression of the poor and the widow, the breaking of God's commandments, the lack of faith, sexual misconduct, selfishness, financial exploitation of the people, and any behavior he found to be senseless and stupid. He called kings, nobles, priests, and other prophets to account for their actions. He makes his case against empty and vain temple-goers who continue to sin and do evil, while never missing a Sabbath or feast day. His message describes a loving, kind and compassionate God who feels great sorrow at having to punish Israel for its sins and its disobedient and unfaithful attitude toward the God of Israel. The Israelites had abandoned God and turned to worshipping foreign gods. Hosea's message has lost none of its relevance in today's world. We know that infidelity is destructive of any relationship not only one with God but with others. Fidelity, loving compassion, and knowledge of God lie at the heart of the covenant relationship. Where Amos saw no hope for Israel, Hosea begged the people to give God a try.

Reflections and Comments

The More things change:

Hosea uses examples from real life to get his point across. He calls on his own life experience to portray just how the northern kingdom, Israel is acting. He sees the relationship between God and Israel in terms of a marriage contract. Israel is guilty of adultery, prostitution, violation of the covenant, infidelity, moral perversion, and complete disregard and indifference for the plight of widows, orphans, aliens, and the poor. Just as in Hosea's own life, his wife was unfaithful to him, so is Israel unfaithful to God. Hosea with God's help was willing to forgive his wife, just as God is willing to forgive Israel, if only they would admit their need for help.

Fidelity, Loving Compassion, Knowledge of God:

Hosea feels that there are three qualities that must be present in any true relationship; faithfulness, empathy, and true knowledge of the other party. Hosea uses striking images and beautiful metaphors to convey his message to his people. It is clear that Hosea felt that his responsibility was to encourage the Israelites to return to the service of their God. Through Moses the people had entered into a covenant relationship with their God. It was as if they had signed a contract which bound them to the service of the Lord. It was a commitment as binding as a marriage contract. Hosea knew from personal experience how devastating rejection, scorn, unfaithfulness, indifference and ingratitude could be. The Israelites were not living up to their contractual obligation. Hosea's use of the marriage metaphor was appropriate for several reasons. Israel had a personal encounter with God. They had spent forty years in the desert getting to know God. While in the desert, God had watched over them, nourished them, led them, listened to their complaints and taken care of them. When Israel became prosperous, they felt that they no longer needed to be faithful. In essence they became an idolatrous nation who attributed their good fortune to a Canaanite god named Baal. Baal was attractive to the people because he was a fertility god who was supposed to guarantee the productivity of land, animals, and people. Instead of giving their allegiance to the one true God they credited Baal with providing the rain, the crops, the oil, the fertility necessary to not only survive but to prosper. In Hosea Chapter 4 verse 1 God says "There is no fidelity, no loyalty, no knowledge of God in the land." He continues to list the crimes that Israel is guilty of committing. The imagery of prostitution and fornication used by Hosea to symbolize idolatry not only fits the circumstances but they fit Hosea's life experience. He had an unfaithful wife who had deserted him, seeking other lovers. God was willing to forgive Israel, if Israel would return to the service of the Lord, and God told Hosea to do the same. Take back your wife, forgive her indiscretion, her rash and inappropriate behavior and do not be troubled. I am the Lord your God and I am kind and merciful and you should follow my example. The level of commitment found in an ideal marriage was the kind of faithfulness Hosea hoped Israel was capable of displaying in their relationship with the God of Israel.

The power of Hosea's message comes in large part from his use of metaphors. "It is love that God desires not sacrifice." Contained in Hosea's Book is a reference to how Jehu had come to power by killing all of Judah's previous leaders. God had requested that Hosea name his first child "Jezreel" which conveys an image of God as one who "sows." It also refers to a valley that the people of Israel would have been familiar with as the place where Jehu, a former king of Israel had slaughtered the previous royal family (2 Kings 10:11). Hosea lets the present rulers know that what they did to the previous administration would not go unpunished. Hosea draws a very clear picture that those who have turned away from the one true God must suffer punishment. It is God who brings the rain, the bread, the wine, and the oil. Once Israel got caught up in worldly concerns their commitment to serve the Lord gradually faded, and the choices they began to make carried unforeseen consequences which ultimately resulted in the punishment Hosea warned would happen. On the surface one is given the impression that Hosea's message is entirely negative. Israel along with their neighbors are guilty of adultery, prostitution, violation of the covenant relationship, infidelity, oppression of the poor and the widow and unfaithfulness to the service of the Lord.

I desire love not sacrifice

The apostle John in his first letter, chapter three and verse eighteen, gets at the heart of what Hosea was trying to say, "Children, let us love not in word or speech but in deed and truth." A true child of God is concerned with the plight of others. Loves begins with the heart, finds fulfillment in knowledge and expression in faithfulness. Hosea's message is John's message that from this day forward you are to be known for your love for God and for each other. In the words of Hosea, "For it is love that I desire, not sacrifice, and knowledge of God rather than holocausts." (Hosea 6:6) A true covenant partner has empathy for others. God wants Israel to love Him as much as He loves Israel. Israel has failed to live up to God's expectations. Hosea's final plea for repentance stresses how God will heal and restore Israel. All they have to do is love God with their hearts and minds and souls as Moses had asked in his farewell speech. Hosea draws a clear comparison between those who turn away from God's law and his own unfaithful wife. Just as Gomer, Hosea's wife dishonored her marriage contract, the people of Israel dishonored their agreement to serve the Lord their God with their whole heart, with their whole mind and with their whole soul, as Moses had directed. God led the Israelites into the desert to separate them from the influences of the world. God wanted the Israelites to be his own people, particularly his own without any worldly interference. In time the people forgot all that God had done for them. Selfishness and greed took precedence over love and concern for others. Hosea confronted a society not unlike the society that exists today. This part of the world has almost always experienced conflict. The killing of Christians, Jews, and others throughout the region is not what God had in mind for his people. The recipe for peace seems so simple. Love God and love your neighbor as yourself. The Middle East has known war and strife for centuries down to the present day. When one adds the prospect of employing nuclear weapons against one's neighbor, the necessity for people to accept God's laws and commandments is obvious. In Jewish Old Testament thought, missing the mark refers to turning away from God. Today's world has turned away from serving God and seeks to honor the world. Indeed, we pay homage to the silly and the senseless, the TV reality shows, the glorifying of immoral behavior, the praise given to athletes, movie stars, and political figures all contribute to distract people from what is truly important. "Pushing the envelope," becomes the phrase justifying the lowering of standards of decency. Hosea saw what lay in store for Judah as they continued on their path of self-destruction. It matters little whether a nation falls from within or from without. When a nation loses its moral compass, it is no longer able to find God. It loses its way. The frustrating thing for Hosea is that it did not have to happen. Today's society does not have to lose its way. Just as Israel refused to repent, i.e. return to the Lord, so our society refuses to listen to the voice of the Lord. "If today you hear the voice of the Lord, harden not your heart." (*Psalm 95:7) Hosea reminded the Israelites just how important God's love is. The primary image of the Book of Hosea is Hosea's marriage, which symbolized the marriage of God and His people. Hosea understood that the leaders, the priests, the prophets and the people were tragically mistaken in their assumption that they knew God. The deficiency in and of itself was tragic enough but the failure to recognize that it existed at all proved to be fatal.

Hosea

Chapter 1	Hosea's Marriage to Gomer
1:1 – 2	Hosea is commissioned by God
1:3	Hosea takes a wife
1:4	A child named "Jezreel"
1: 5 – 9	More children are named

Chapter 2	Punishment and Restoration
2:4 – 7	Indictment of the faithless wife
2:10 – 15	Israel's ingratitude renounced
2:8 – 9	Imprisoned by her own behavior
2:16 – 20	Reconciliation offered
2:21 – 25	Redemption possible

Chapter 3	Triumph of Love
3:1 – 4	A faithful husband
3:5 – 3	Hope for the future

Chapter 4	Israel's Guilt and Punishment
4:1 – 3	I will punish all your iniquities
4:4 – 19	The guilt of the priests

Chapter 5   **The Guilt of the Leaders**

5:1 – 4   They do not recognize the Lord
5:5 – 7   Israel is convicted of arrogance
5:8 – 14   Political upheaval condemned
5:15   Insincere conversion punished

Chapter 6   **False Repentance**

6:1 – 6   It is love that I desire
6:7 – 11   They violate my covenant

Chapter 7   **The Guilt of Ephraim revealed**

7:1 – 2   They do not understand
7:3 – 7   Israel's political wickedness
7:8 – 12   They make foreign alliances
7:13 – 16   Woe to Israel for straying

Chapter 8   **They No Longer seek my Approval**

8:1 – 6   Samaria will be destroyed
8:7 – 14   Israel has forgotten their God

Chapter 9   **Days of Punishment are Coming**

9:1 – 6   God rejects your sacrifices
9:7 – 9   God will punish your sins
9:10 – 14   They turned their backs on God

| 9:15 – 17 | For the crime of Gilgal I disown them |

Chapter 10   The Sin of Idolatry

10:1 – 6	Their heart is false
10:7 – 10	I will chastise them for their sins
10:11 – 15	Time to seek the Lord

Chapter 11   God's Love for Israel Recalled

| 11:1 – 7 | Israel refuses to repent |
| 11:8 – 11 | God will bring their exile to an end |

Chapter 12   Israel's Rebellion Continues

12:1 – 7	Return to the Lord
12:8 – 12	Enough of your falsehood
12:13 – 15	Moses brought you out of Egypt

Chapter 13   The Death of Ephraim

13:1 – 3	Punishment for ingratitude
13:4 – 6	I am the Lord your God
13:7 – 11	From where will your help come
13:12 – 15	I shall loot the land

Chapter 14   Samaria Shall Fall by the Sword

| 14:1 | Everything will be taken from you |

14:2 – 4	Return to the Lord
14:5 – 8	There is hope for the future
14:9 – 10	Let him who is wise understand

The New American Bible: pages 981 – 991
Copyright: Catholic Publishers, Inc. 1971
A Division of Thomas Nelson, Inc.

CHAPTER FOUR

The Prophet
Isaiah

Isaiah

Our fourth prophet for study is Isaiah. He is one of the four Major Prophets. The terms "major" and "minor" refer to the length of the respective compositions and not to their relative importance. Isaiah is one of the most frequently quoted and readily recognizable of the sixteen prophets. The Book of Isaiah opens with a listing of the kings of Judah with whom Isaiah interacted. They were Uzziah, Jotham, Ahaz and Hezekiah. They ruled Judah from 783 B.C. to 686 B.C. The Book of Isaiah covers over one hundred and forty years of Jewish history. He expresses the same outrage found in Amos and Hosea regarding oppression and injustice. He matches their denunciations of idolatry and violations of covenant. He berates the vain worship and shallow religious ritualism practiced by the people of the Judah kingdom. He shares the bitter anguish expressed by Hosea as he begged the Israelites to return to the service of God. What makes Isaiah unique, in my opinion, is his focus on the big picture of God's plan of salvation for the whole universe. Isaiah's vision of the future is one of hope, when a new king will lead the people back to the service of the Lord and do God's will. He sees a Messiah who will save the world and all the people have to do is listen to the voice of God. "If today you hear the voice of the Lord, harden not your hearts." (*Psalm 95:8) Moses called upon heaven and earth to witness the unfaithfulness of the Israelites in their desert journey. (Deuteronomy 4:25-26). Isaiah opens his book calling upon heaven and earth to witness just how far astray the Israelites have wandered away from the service of the Lord. Dumb animals appreciate their dependence upon their masters and yet the Israelites fail to acknowledge just how much God has done for them. The people of Judah are guilty of blatant covenant violations. They have forsaken the Lord. Isaiah compares them to Sodom and Gomorrah. He tells them that God has grown weary of their worthless offerings. It is a time to fly right. A time to get back on track. A time to wake up. A time to put their misdeeds behind them and a time to set things right. Failure to do so will result in dire consequences. One of the major indictments made by Isaiah is the belief that the Israelites could go through the motions of true worship and righteous behavior without harming their relationship with God. God repeatedly rejects this notion. The prophets make it clear that the people have turned their backs on God. God makes it perfectly clear that they lack due respect. God finds their half-hearted, lukewarm, hypocritical worship annoying. If they truly loved God they would take care of the widow, the orphan, the foreigner, the weak and the poor. Through Isaiah God stands in judgment of Israel and Judah. They have been found wanting and yet judgment and punishment is not what God intended for his people. Isaiah injects the "vineyard song" into his message. What more could God have done for his vineyard? His vineyard, his people have not turned out as they should have turned out. They have borne fruit unworthy of their high calling. Their behavior does not live up to the expectations and standards that one associates with God's people. God will no longer protect Israel from foreign invasion. This story unfolds gradually as historical events take shape within Isaiah's composition. Chapter 5, verse 26 describes the process. Isaiah interrupts his discussion of unfolding events in Chapter 6 to describe his call to be a prophet for God. Isaiah sees the Lord seated on his throne. "Holy, holy, holy is the Lord of hosts!" Isaiah recognizes that he does not belong in the presence of the Lord. "Woe is me, I am doomed!" (Isaiah 6:5) The angel cleaned his lips with an ember and purged his wickedness. Isaiah answers the Lord's question and never looks back. "Here I am," he said, "send me!" God tells Isaiah He will tell him what to say, but he should realize the people are not going to listen to what he has to say. God tells him not to become discouraged; a lot of bad things are going to happen and yet there is reason to hope. The stage is set. In our comments on the prophet Jonah we discussed the prediction made by Jonah of the expansion and prosperity of Israel and Judah. This leads to an alliance between Israel and Damascus which in turn leads to a threat of war against Judah. A simple remark made by Jonah in the Book of Kings ultimately results in a warning made by Isaiah to Ahaz, the king of Judah, not to enter into an alliance with a foreign power. It is with the death of Uzziah, king of Judah, that events begin to unfold which will lead to the inviting of Assyria into the area for protection against Israel and Damascus which results in the destruction of Samaria and the siege of Jerusalem. Isaiah lived through the rise to power of Assyria. He was given the privilege of seeing into the future. Isaiah sees God as the "Holy One of Israel." Isaiah tells the people that a child is to be born. This specific prediction is connected to a conversation Isaiah had with Ahaz, king of Judah, regarding the ill-advised treaty with Assyria. Isaiah asked Ahaz to ask God for a sign to show how powerful God is and how foolish it would be to enter into an alliance with Assyria. Ahaz refuses to ask God for a sign because he had already decided to make the alliance. God gives Ahaz a sign of a child anyway: "The virgin shall be with child, and bear a son and shall name him Immanuel." (Isaiah 7:14) Isaiah's role in God's plan of salvation was to draw attention to the fact that Israel was being held accountable for its behavior. God stands in judgment over the nations. God is sovereign and all creation is subject to the laws of God, the creator. Everyone and everything will be judged at the proper time. Isaiah's message is more than judgment and righteous punishment. It offers hope; a promise of deliverance and future restoration to all who are willing to listen to the word of the Lord. There are a ton of clichés one might use to describe the point that Isaiah is attempting to make. "It is always darkest before the dawn." "There is light at the end of the tunnel." "This storm will pass." "Things could be worse!" Isaiah's message is quite clear. Israel has sinned and they need to repent. Failure to repent leads to judgment and punishment and yet there is reason for optimism; God will bring Israel back to life. It is never too late, short of death, to return to the service of the Lord. Isaiah proclaimed his message in Jerusalem. He is believed to have had a royal connection and was welcomed into the power structure of his day. Isaiah saw the destruction of Samaria, the siege of Jerusalem, the defeat of Assyria, the rise of Babylon, the destruction of the temple in Jerusalem, the taking of the survivors into exile, and lastly the return of the exiles to rebuild Jerusalem and the temple. He recognized his own unworthiness to proclaim God's message to his people and yet he volunteered to do the work of the Lord. From the very beginning he warned Israel not to become involved in foreign alliances. Put your faith in God and He will take care of you. The people failed to heed God's warning. The book of Isaiah is filled with vivid images of God's holiness, power and sovereignty. Isaiah's writings focus upon God's plan for the entire world. Put your trust in God. Isaiah was familiar with the oppression and the injustice visited upon the poor. He had the same intense anger as Amos and Hosea had demonstrated. Isaiah knew that the time of testing which Israel would undergo would be long and difficult. Had the people remained faithful to their commitment to the covenant all of this pain and suffering could have been avoided. Nevertheless, the book of Isaiah contains reason to hope. God will not abandon his people. There will be better days ahead. The prophet Isaiah is often considered the greatest of the Old Testament prophets. His message on the one hand is one of pain and suffering for the people's disobedience and failure to listen to the voice of God. On the other hand, his message contains an element of hope for a brighter future. One of the major complaints leveled against Israel and Judah was their religious ritualism. They believed that they could go through the motions ignoring true worship and righteous behavior. God makes it clear that he is unhappy with their "worship" activities. He is annoyed with their insincerity and he no longer listens to their prayers. Isaiah's message is stop doing evil, learn to do good. Isaiah points out Israel's and Judah's sinfulness, their violations against the covenant, the disingenuous and hypocritical religious ritualism, their disregard for social justice, their treatment of the poor, the widow and the orphan, their lack of faith and their lip service. Israel and Judah ignored Isaiah's advice. Isaiah turns his attention to the future when a king, who will obey God, will appear and show the people the way back to the service of the Lord. The beautiful visions of Immanuel were Isaiah's way of showing that God would stand by his people if they remain faithful to the service of the Lord. The true importance of Isaiah does not depend upon whether he was successful in changing the thinking of the kings and the people during his lifetime. His words contain that rare mix of ethical insight realistic warning of disaster to come, and long-ranged hopefulness as a reward for faithfulness.

Reflections and Comments

Images found in Isaiah:

Hope for the future is one of the themes that is stressed by Isaiah. In chapter 7, 8, and 9 Isaiah shares the expectation and sign of a special child that is to come. The child's name is "Immanuel." (Isaiah 7:14) The child is connected to the messianic hope of a great king who is to come. His name "God with us" has merged into a spectacular promise, a foreshadowing of the ultimate fulfillment that is found in the New Testament. In a very real sense we are still awaiting the return of the child who will come at the end of time. He will establish a world of peace and justice.

Judgment on the nations:

Isaiah 13 – 23 is made up of observations involving Israel's neighbors pointing out the political intrigue, the arrogant disregard for human life, the treatment of the poor, the widow, the orphan, the foreigner, and the failure to acknowledge God's sovereignty. "The earth is polluted because of its inhabitants, who have transgressed laws, violated statutes, broken the ancient covenant" (Isaiah 24:5)

A sign will be given:

"the virgin shall be with child, and bear a son, and shall name him Immanuel." (Isaiah 7:14) Isaiah had warned Ahaz not to enter into an alliance with Assyria. God wanted to give Ahaz a sign which he refused to accept. The entire point was to trust in God not in others. Their armies, their charioteers, their horses, their weapons are nothing in the eyes of God. Put your faith in God. The Lord alone is able to save you if you but trust in Him.

On Eagle's wings:

Chapter 40 of Isaiah proclaims "Comfort" to Jerusalem and an end to her punishment is announced. Isaiah sees the hand of God guiding the exiles in Babylon back to glory. The Lord will lift up the remnant of Israel and return them to the land of their forefathers. The glory of God will be revealed. All of the nations that have caused suffering for God's people are as nothing in the eyes of God. Therefore,

God's people should not despair or be despondent, but rather soar like eagles for the time of renewal is coming.

The Servant of the Lord:

Who is this servant? The first servant song is Isaiah 42:1-4. The second servant song is Isaiah 49:1-6. The third servant song is Isaiah 50:4-9. The forth servant song is Isaiah 52:13. This servant of the Lord speaks God's words, is abused, is rejected, is plotted against, and manifests God's goodness before all the nations of the earth. Scholars have suggested that this servant is an individual, perhaps Moses, or David, or Elijah, or one of the prophets, or an ideal composite. The New Testament writers recognized Jesus as the true servant. Just as Israel suffered in the Old Testament as a witness and light to the world, the New Testament authors saw in Jesus through his crucifixion and suffering one willing to redeem all the nations coming to do the will of the Father. For Christians it is just as legitimate to see in the person of the servant the key to understanding Christ's suffering, death and resurrection as the redemption for all the nations no matter what Isaiah intended to demonstrate.

The Messiah's Mission:

The lord has "sent me to bring glad tidings to the lowly, to proclaim liberty to the captives and release to the prisoners," (Isaiah 61:1). Jesus quotes the words of Isaiah to describe his mission. Jesus comes to do the will of the Father and save his people from their sins.

The Corporal Works of Mercy:

Isaiah 58:7 "Sharing your bread with the hungry, sheltering the oppressed and the homeless; Clothing the naked…" Feed the hungry; give drink to the thirsty; Clothe the naked; shelter the homeless; visit the sick; visit the imprisoned; and bury the dead. The Christian obligation is to do these things for the least of their brothers and sisters for in so doing they do it for Christ. It is Jesus who will have the final victory.

Some final comments:

Isaiah's message is as relevant today as when it was first uttered. His prophecies are detailed, pertinent, and thought-provoking. He quotes Moses pointing out that behavior has consequences. The disobedient are like a tree with falling leaves, like a garden that has no water. Isaiah reinforces the message expressed by Hosea and Amos. God will hold those who have much responsible for the care of the poor, the orphan, the foreigner, and the widow, to account. Isaiah told the leaders of Israel and Judah that they must speak the truth and stand up for what is right. There is an Archbishop in the West cut in the mold of Isaiah speaking the truth and calling on the Church to stand up for what is right. Catholic educators should do their job. Teach the truth, stand up for what is right and do what is pleasing in the sight of God. God warned Isaiah that the people would not listen to him and things have not changed in today's world. Isaiah would recognize that our society has the same problems he had to deal with in his day. Wealth has been concentrated into the hands of a few individuals who relish the idea of being wealthy and put their opulence of display. Isaiah asked the leaders to be true to the service of the Lord. As difficult as he found his society to be, he believed that there was reason to hope. His message was profound and yet quite simple. Return to the service of the Lord, do good works, take care of those in need. Trust in the Lord! How is it possible to know the Lord and still sin? How is it possible to know the Lord and still turn one's back on the poor? How is it possible to know the Lord and refuse to be true to oneself? There is no doubt that God will have the final victory!

Isaiah

Chapter 1 to 5   **Covenant violations**

    1:2 – 16   Heaven and earth bear witness
    2:6 – 12   Judgment against idols
    3:9 – 15   Judgment of Judah and Jerusalem
    5:8 – 16   Oracles of reproach

Chapters 6 to 12   **Immanuel prophecies**

    6:1 – 13   Call of Isaiah
    7:10 – 17   Birth of Immanuel
    8:1 – 23   Trust in God not foreign alliances
    9:1-6   A light will shine (Matt 4:-12)
    9:15 – 20   The fall of Samaria
    10:1 – 4   Social injustice
    10:28 – 34   Sennacherib's invasion
    11:1 – 9   The promise of a king to come
    12:I – 6   A song of thanksgiving

Chapters 13 to 23   **Oracles against the pagan nations**

    13:1 – 14:23   Babylon
    14:24 – 27   Assyria
    14:28 – 32   Philistia
    15:1 – 16:14   Moab
    17:1 – 11   Damascus
    18:1 – 7   Ethiopia/Cush

19:1 – 25	Egypt
20:1 – 6	Captivity of Egypt and Ethiopia
21:1 – 10	The fall of Babylon
21:11 – 12	Edom
21:13 – 17	Arabia
22:1 – 25	Jerusalem
23:1 – 18	Tyre and Sidon

Chapters 24 to 27 A remnant saved

24:1 – 17	Judgment on the earth
25:1 – 9	Praise the name of the Lord
26:4 – 11	Trust in the Lord forever
27:13	The day of deliverance

Chapters 28 to 35 The Lord is Israel's salvation

28:1 – 6	The fate of Samaria
29:2 – 8	The fall of Jerusalem
29:13 – 16	Religious ritualism
29:17 – 24	A day of redemption
30:1 – 7	Do not trust in foreign alliances
30:18 – 26	Trust only in the Lord
31:1 – 9	Egypt and Assyria will fall
32:9 – 20	The woman of Jerusalem addressed
33:1 – 8	The overthrow of Assyria
34:1 – 8	Judgment on the nations
35:3 – 10	Israel's deliverance

Chapters 36 to 39   Historical appendix

36:1 – 21	The invasion of Sennacherib
37:21 – 32	A prayer is answered
37:33 – 38	Jerusalem is saved by the Lord
38:1 – 7	Illness and recovery
38:9 – 20	A prayer of thanksgiving
39:3 – 8	Isaiah warns Hezekiah

Chapters 40 to 55   Hope and restoration

40:1 – 5	A promise of salvation
40:12 – 31	How great is our God
41:10 – 20	Fear not I am with you
42: 1 – 9	The servant of the Lord
42:10 – 23	Sing a new song to the Lord
43:1 – 21	Promises of redemption
44:6 – 25	True and false gods
45:1 – 3	Cyrus the Persian king
45:18 – 21	I am the Lord there is no other
46:8 – 9	Remember this!
47:11 – 15	The fall of Babylon
48:20 – 22	The end of exile

Chapters 49 to 55   Spiritual liberation of Israel

49:1 – 7	The servant of the Lord
49:8 – 14	God's plan for salvation
49:15 – 26	I will never forget you
50:4 – 11	The Lord God is my help

Richard C. Kelley and Leo F. Peterson

51:1 – 6	Trust in the Lord
52:13 – 53:12	The final servant song
54:4 – 10	The new Zion
55:1 – 3	An invitation to grace

Chapters 56 to 66 Return of the Captives

56:1 – 8	The Lord's house open to all
57:1 – 13	The failure of Israel's leaders
58:1 – 7	True fasting will be rewarded
59:2 – 8	Your sin is your problem
60:2 – 3	A brighter day is coming
60:19 – 21	The Lord will be your light
61:1 – 3	The Messiah mission glad tidings
61:4 – 11	The reward of Israel
62:1 – 5	Nations behold your vindication
62:6 – 12	Jerusalem will be re-established
63:1 – 6	The punishment of Edom
63:7 – 19	Prayer for the return of God's favor
64:7 – 11	A final plea
65:1 – 7	You know me and yet you still sin
65:8 – 16	The good and the bad in Israel
66:1 – 6	True and false worship
66:22 – 24	The Lord's final victory

The New American Bible: pages 777 – 840
Copyright: Catholic Publishers, Inc. 1971
A Division of Thomas Nelson, Inc.

CHAPTER FIVE

The Prophet
Micah

Micah

Micah, our fifth prophet, was active in the eighth century. He saw the same injustices, neglect and evil that his contemporaries witnessed. Micah's message was powerful and uncompromising. He declared that even if the entire nation should become corrupt and turn away from God, he will be faithful to the Lord, he will wait patiently and trust only in the Lord. A hundred years later his words would be used by Jeremiah in his defense of his prophecy against the kingdom. If Micah could warn Israel about their impending doom, certainly Jeremiah would be within his rights to do the same thing. Micah received no punishment for his words against Israel and Judah and neither should Jeremiah. Jeremiah's defense prevailed. His message was and is truthful and it has stood the test of time. Micah attacked the rich, the exploiters of the poor, fraudulent merchants, corrupt judges, dishonest priests and prophets. His charges were leveled against the landlords who took advantage of the poor and he foresaw the same judgment coming upon the people and their leaders that Isaiah saw. Micah points the finger of God directly at Samaria and Jerusalem. God is planning to bring destruction on Israel. They will be held accountable for their behavior and punishment will be measured out to them. One group that Micah singled out for their misdeeds were the prophets. They were inclined to tell the people what they wanted to hear: "Everything is fine, there is no reason to worry." They tailored their message to their market. "Be happy, don't worry." They were leading the people astray. Micah was not just a negative prognosticator of bad news. He told the people what they needed to hear. He told the people what God wanted them to know. He told them the truth. Micah did see that a new day was coming. Following their punishment, God will rebuild the walls of their city and breathe life into the empty ruins of the land. God would not abandon his people. Micah describes the future restoration as a time of peace, a time when "They shall beat their swords into plowshares, and their spears into pruning hooks." (Micah 4:3) In chapter 5, Micah proclaims the coming of one who will be a shepherd and who will establish peace for his people. Matthew chapter 2; verse 3, relates how King Herod summoned the chief priests and scribes inquiring of them where the Messiah was to be born. They told him Bethlehem quoting the prophet Micah. Micah's message was simple and to the point. If the people do not repent God will punish them severely. However, after a period of purification, a new light of hope will shine out for God's people. Judah, which is smaller than Israel, missed the advantages and avoided the dangers of Samaria. Samaria was on the main trade route which connected Asia and Africa. It was this fact that brought wealth and material prosperity to her people. Prosperity diverted Israel's attention away from service to the Lord. Moses had warned the people not to get caught in the ways of their neighbors or imitate their behavior. Judah and Jerusalem, nestled behind her foothills, managed to escape the spotlight of international trade and remain relatively unnoticed outside her borders. Thus Samaria became a target for intrigue and conquest. Micah knew that is was a matter of time before

Samaria would be destroyed. He warned them and they failed to listen. Little is known of Micah's personal life. His preaching focused upon sin and punishment, not political or cultic matters. He is preoccupied with social justice and he holds no fear of princes, prophets, people or priests in his heart. Micah is concerned with the people's violation of the Mosaic covenant. Micah condemns Samaria and Jerusalem. Their sins are the reason that divine punishment is on the horizon. Their leaders mistake evil for good and good for evil. Some bad stuff is about to befall Israel and Judah. The sad part of all this is the fact that it could have been avoided. Their leaders accepted bribes, their merchants stole from and cheated the poor, even their religious worship lacked sincerity. In the midst of all this, Micah inserted a note of hope in the middle of his book. It is very likely that Micah and his contemporary Isaiah shared a cup of tea as they discussed what lie in store for God's people. Jerusalem survived nearly a century and a half after the fall and destruction of Samaria. Judah and Jerusalem got into trouble when they meddled in the affairs of other nations. Micah was not concerned with international affairs. What aroused his bitter indignation was their loss of a sense of sinfulness, their lack of faith, their refusal to walk with the Lord and their arrogance devoid of all humility. The book of Micah is very similar to Isaiah only much shorter. Micah 4:1 – 3 is almost identical to Isaiah 2:1 – 4. Both of them lived in Jerusalem and were aware of each other's ministry. Micah proclaimed that God was disappointed with his people. They were not living the kind of life that was pleasing to God. What God wanted from his people was not so much material offerings, as acts of humility, justice and charity. He wanted his people to acknowledge their dependency upon God their creator. People in positions of authority used their power to force people out of their homes and family farms because of the greed of their leaders. They had become part of the world with all its anxieties, worries and concerns. They had come to believe that they could not be touched as long as the temple of God was present in Jerusalem. They had seen Samaria destroyed. The city of Jerusalem had been surrounded by the Assyrian leader Sennacherib in 701 B.C. and yet they had been delivered from the hands of their enemy. The fact that they felt they could not be touched contributed to their complacency and their sense of pride and conceit. They believed that they had been delivered by the hand of God, when a plague struck Sennacherib's army and he had to withdraw. When the threat of destruction was removed, their commitment to serve the Lord vanished and they believed that they were free to behave as their desires directed them. Micah's love for his God shown through the words that he wrote and cried out that the people return to the service of the Lord.

Reflections and Comments

True Sacrifice:

Micah reminds the people that God is not impressed with the number of sacrifices, but rather the quality. God desires that his people do justice, that they love and are loyal, that they walk humbly and engage in a daily relationship with their God. This advice is as relevant today as when Micah first stated it. God is much more concerned that his people are actively involved in bringing about justice than he is about ritualistic worship and meaningless pomp and circumstance. God desires that his people acknowledge their dependence upon him in their daily existence. Here we take a lesson from the universe. Each day the universe gives witness and praise to the living God. Should we do anything less?

Compassion:

The book of Micah resembles the book of Isaiah in a number of ways. Isaiah is not known for his brevity and while there are similarities between the two, Micah's book is shorter. Both authors take Israel to task for their lack of compassion. Why are you planning evil at night on your beds? Why are you defrauding people of their lands and houses? Who do you think gave the people their land to begin with, was it not God? Why are you doing all this "bad stuff" even to the point of harming your children? Do you not realize that God will hold you accountable? Do you believe that you can operate without impunity? Micah declares that just as Israel and Judah acted without compassion, God is planning to return the favor. "Therefore thus says the Lord: Behold, I am planning against this race an evil from which you shall not withdraw your necks." (Micah 2:3)

Like sheep without a shepherd:

Micah decries the lack of leadership. The leaders are corrupt, the priests are looking out for themselves, the false prophets say only what they know the people want to hear and the people have lost their way. Micah declares that a true shepherd is coming. He will be born in Bethlehem and people will not have to try to figure out where He stands: "He shall stand firm and shepherd his flock by the strength of the Lord." (Micah 5:3)

Trust in the Lord:

At the end of his book, Micah returns to the theme of hope and future restoration. "But as for me, I will look to the Lord, I will put my trust in God my Savior;" (Micah 7:7)

Micah

Chapter 1 to 3   **Impending judgment on Israel**

1:1	A brief introduction
1:2 – 7	The sins of Israel and Judah
1:8 – 15	Invasion is coming
1:16	A time for mourning
2:1 – 5	Woe to those who plot evil
2:6 – 11	The people are being led astray
2:12-13	A future restoration is predicted
3.1 – 4	The downfall of present leaders
3:5 – 12	A word to false prophets

Chapter 4 to 5   **The new Israel**

4:1 – 7	A promise of things to come
4:8 – 14	Babylonian captivity predicted
5:1 – 3	Israel's future ruler (the Messiah)
5:4 – 6	The ultimate fate of Assyria
5:7 – 14	The remnant of Jacob

Chapter 6 to 7   **Admonish**

6:1 – 4	The case against Israel
6:6 – 7	Accusation and answer
6:8 – 12	You should know what God wants

6:13 – 16	Because of your sins I will strike you
7:1 – 6	Things go from bad to worse
7:7 – 13	Trust in the Lord
7:14 – 15	Shepherd your people
7:16 – 17	Put your confidence in God
7:18 – 20	Who is like our God?

The New American Bible: pages 1010 – 1016
Copyright: Catholic Publishers, Inc. 1971
A Division of Thomas Nelson, Inc.

CHAPTER SIX

The Prophet
Nahum

Nahum

Nahum is the sixth prophet in our study. His overall message is one of the future violent destruction of the city of Nineveh. In today's world, Nahum's writings are not seen as compelling or as relevant as they once were. This is unfortunate since Nahum's view of God is as important today as it has ever been. He pictures God as a divine warrior who comes to rescue his people. God cannot be conquered, nor will he abandon his people. In chapter two of his writings, Nahum describes God's enemies as fierce lions who will have their teeth pulled, as harlot sorceresses who will be humiliated in public, as locusts who will be destroyed. This enemy has had a stranglehold on the world and on God's people in particular for long enough. Nahum describes the suffering and the hardship God's people have had to endure at the hand of the Ninevehites. Their time has come to an end and God will administer proper justice. They will be burned as stubble, eaten as a ripe fig and consumed as a cup of judgment spilled upon the ground. His book is a colorful, imaginative and creative text of the Old Testament. It consists of three chapters. Clearly there is no love lost between Nahum and the city of Nineveh, the capital of the Assyrian empire. His book hides none of his angry and impassioned hatred held against Assyria. They were a cruel people who had a history of dealing harshly with foreigners and with Israel in particular. Nahum details how Assyria will be cut down, lose her political influence, have her temples and idols destroyed and her people put to the sword. Nahum points out that the repentance experienced by Nineveh's inhabitants over one hundred and fifty years earlier with Jonah was short-lived. Shortly after Jonah's disappointment, i.e. the repentance of the people in the city of Nineveh, Assyria began its rise to prominence and power. Ultimately, they dominated the Near East, defeating Damascus, Israel, Egypt and their surrounding neighbors. They established their dominance over Judah. God used Assyria to judge and punish Israel and Judah. They failed to listen to the Lord and without realizing what they had done, they turned their backs on the Lord. The basic message of Nahum is that the time for judgment and punishment has come to Nineveh. "Till everyone who sees you runs from you, saying, "Nineveh is destroyed; who can pity her?" (Nahum 2:7) All that will be left will be a pile of sand. The prophet Jonah had hoped to see the destruction of Nineveh nearly one hundred and fifty years earlier. The fact that it finally happened gave Judah hope that they were out of danger and that God would protect them. The Assyrian army under Sennacherib did indeed manage to surround the city of Jerusalem in 701 B.C. The Assyrian army was devastated with illness and the king had to withdraw his army. The people of Judah believed that the God of Israel had rescued them from destruction. This incident in their history convinced them that they did not have to live as God wanted them to live because no matter what, God would not allow the city of Jerusalem to be touched. Unfortunately, during the lifetime of Jeremiah the city of Jerusalem was destroyed by the Babylonians. The basic message of the book of Nahum is judgment on Nineveh. Just as Jonah had pointed out, all nations are held accountable to God. If you repent you will be forgiven. On the other hand, if you relapse you will be punished. "God is slow to anger and great in power; He will not leave the guilty unpunished." (Nahum 1:3) Throughout the history of mankind we see the pattern repeated. There is a gradual rise to power. There is a high point, a golden age achieved and a gradual decline. Nineveh is but one example of that pattern as it plays out over and over in the Middle East. Assyria is followed by Babylon, who is followed by Persia and the Medes, who are followed by the Greeks, who are followed by the Romans. Decay develops from within and is fostered by the loss of one's moral compass and a turning away from the service of the Lord. God's people whether Jew or Christian seem to bear the brunt of animosity and hatred. The book of Nahum is directed at the citizens of Nineveh. Nahum refers to the fall of Thebes as a past event thus marking his ministry after that date. Nahum presents the other side of the coin. The preaching of the prophets had primarily focused upon the behavior of Israel and Judah. Nahum presents God's concern with the behavior of foreign nations. Just as God had used Assyria to administer judgment upon Israel and Judah, so Nineveh will be judged by the Medes and the Babylonians. The city of Nineveh was taken in three months. The city was looted and was turned into a pile of debris and sand. When Nineveh was destroyed, it was never rebuilt. For centuries the location of the city of Nineveh was unknown, so complete had been its destruction. It was discovered in 1845 A.D. by archeologists. God's prophecies of judgment may be delayed but in God's good time they will be fulfilled. Jonah would have been pleased. All those who had been conquered by Assyria rejoiced at its defeat. Like Jonah, Nahum does not address Israel directly. He speaks to the people of Nineveh. He encourages them to repent, just as Jonah had done one hundred and fifty years earlier. Unfortunately, their time had run out and it was now the time for judgment. Nahum's message is twofold: God is sovereign and there is a time for judgment. God cannot be ignored, manipulated or controlled in any way. In the cultures of the Middle East there were numerous gods. In the ancient world, gods were linked to territory and place, which easily escapes the modern reader. There were gods of the state government, national gods, gods of the home, gods of peace and gods of war, gods of the neighborhood; there were gods for every event and occasion. Manipulation and control of these gods by any means necessary would lead to an advantage that was envied and was sought after. The first commandment warns against attempting to manipulate or control the God of Israel. Nahum's point is that God is sovereign, and we are all to be held accountable for our actions. The God of Israel is the God of all creation. No one is above the commandments of the God of Israel. We will all be held accountable.

Reflections and Comments

God will look after his own:

In the Old Testament there are numerous examples of how the God of Israel rescued his people from difficult circumstances. There is the story of Elijah's contest with the prophets of Baal

(1 Kings 19:18). In 2 Chronicles 32:21, we read how the Lord protected Jerusalem in response to Hezekiah's prayer. There is the story of Daniel in the lion's den, the story of Jeremiah in the muddy well and of course the story of the young men in the fiery furnace. In every story, those who remained faithful to the Lord were not abandoned.

Atonement:

The Old Testament concept of atonement presupposes two parties that are estranged, with an act of atonement being the means of reconciling them and bringing about a state of harmony. Atonement is thus a solution to the main problem of the human race, i.e. estrangement from God. "Without the shedding of blood there is no forgiveness of sins." In the 1960's it was announced that the concept of sin served no useful purpose and should be retired from our vocabulary. Is it any wonder that people feel they are under no obligation to atone to God for past transgressions?

Accountability:

In the Old Testament the prevailing view is that the human person is a flawed being and given enough time will do something that is not in their own best interest. The inhabitants of Nineveh were no exception. The story of Adam and Eve, the story of Cain and Abel, the story of the big flood, the story of the Assyrians, the Babylonians, the Persians, the Greeks, and the Romans all end with the decay and downfall of individuals and empires that at one time were thought to be powerful and invincible. The lesson that the prophets bring to all people is that what is truly important is how one stands in the eyes of God. God is sovereign. God is kind and merciful. All people will be held accountable for their actions. There is hope that all things will work for good if we just open our ears to hear God's words and respond with humility. The prophets chose to serve God. Moral decay has caused the decline and downfall of many empires and powers in the world. Return to the service of the Lord! The Middle East is a part of the world that has always witnessed turmoil and conflict. In many ways the history of humankind is the story of people behaving badly. In Nahum's world there were beheading, crucifixions and bodies being burned; these behaviors are happening today.

Nahum

Chapter 1   **God's patience and power**

1:1   Nahum's prophecy
1:2   A jealous and avenging God
1:3   Slow to anger
1:4 – 8   God's terrifying appearance
1:9 – 11   Nineveh's judgment has arrived
1:12 – 14   You shall be a pile of sand

Chapter 2   **Judah's vindication**

2:1   Let Judah celebrate
2:2 – 3   The honor of Judah of Israel restored
2:4 – 10   The attack on Nineveh described
2:11 – 12   Emptiness, desolation and waste
2:13 – 14   The lion is destroyed

Chapter 3   **Ruin imminent and inevitable**

3:1 – 5   I will punish all your iniquities
3:6 – 7   Nineveh is judged
3:8 – 10   Are you better than Thebes?
3:11 – 15   Your city will be destroyed
3:16 – 18   Your fate is inescapable
3:19   Nations will rejoice at the news

The New American Bible: pages 1017 – 1019
Copyright: Catholic Publishers, Inc. 1971
A Division of Thomas Nelson, Inc

Chapter Seven

The Prophet Zephaniah

Zephaniah

Our seventh prophet is Zephaniah who was active during the reign of Josiah, king of Judah. Zephaniah was a fiery preacher whose wrath against Israel's pagan practices and his hatred of Assyria were matched only by his devotion to God and his service to the Lord. As with the other prophets, we know very little about him. He repeats the theme expressed by Isaiah, eighty years earlier. A day of judgment is coming when the Lord will punish Israel for their sins against God and humankind. A time is coming when there will be a period of purification for sins committed by the nations and by the covenant people, namely the Israelities. Zephaniah recognized that he was dealing with a nearly hopeless situation. Jewish society was filled with corruption, religious ritualism, false worship practices and a people in need of repentance. The people had lost their sense of morality. The Leaders were neglecting their duties and their allegiance had been given to the highest bidder. The shepherds were failing to lead the people in a call for humility, faith and faithfulness. The "Day of Judgment" was a day pictured in chapter one of his writings as a time of darkness, a day of anguish and distress, a day of destruction and devastation and a day of threat to the very existence of all animals and humans. People were oblivious to what was going to happen as in the days of Noah when he entered the ark and the rains came. Zephaniah holds Judah to account for their worship of other deities and for its unjust and abusive leadership. He warns the people of

Judah first and he preaches just as boldly against foreign nations predicting that the same fate will fall upon them. He tells them that God will humble the Philistines, the Cretans, the Ammonites, the Cushites, the Egyptians and the Assyrians. The destruction of Nineveh is placed at the end of the list because their crimes against God's people was greater than any of the other nations. Zephaniah's book is composed of two major sections. The first part deals with the oracles against Judah and foreign nations calling for judgment and punishment. The second part describes the promise of things to come. There will be a time of blessing on the faithful remnant of Judah along with those Gentiles from among the nations who come to worship God. The closing verse of Zephaniah summarizes the promises of God's blessing upon those who return to the service of the Lord. "At that time I will bring you home and at that time I will gather you;" (Zephaniah 3:20). Whatever the Lord promises the Lord will do! The book of Zephaniah ends on a positive note. Zephaniah's ministry occurred during the reign of Josiah king of Judah. The kings that preceded and those who followed Josiah were not very good examples of rulers of God's people. Without exception they all turned their backs on the Lord. Zephaniah attempted to bring them back to the service of the Lord. He received his commission from God and was asked to stir the conscience of the people of Judah. All genuine prophets speak as God's personal representatives.

Having been selected, commissioned and sent by him they became God's mouthpieces. Failure to listen to the prophet was a failure to listen to God. Whether Zephaniah was aware of how long it would be until the day of the Lord would arrive was unimportant. What mattered was whether the people recognized that the "Day of Judgment" was inevitable. This coming day will be a time of judgment on rebellious Judah, as well as on the surrounding nations that ignored God to their own peril. Zephaniah used colorful phrases to describe the "Day of the Lord." A "day of trouble and distress," a "day of destruction and desolation," a "day of darkness and gloom," and a "day of trumpet and battle cry," to list but a few examples. Zephaniah's message can be summed up in terms of its announcement of the "Day of the Lord." While the people of Judah believed that this day would be a day of vindication for the Jewish people. Zephaniah made it abundantly clear to all who were willing to listen to him, that this was not the case. This day was one of invitation to do penance extended to the pagan nations and aimed directly at Judah specifically. A day of divine judgment against sinners would come bringing death and destruction if the people did not repent. No matter how serious their sin, if they would but trust in God they would be spared the pain and suffering to be visited upon those who refused to repent. A faithful remnant would be given new hope and confidence and a promise of salvation to be found in the Messiah who was coming to set things right. Zephaniah called on all humble and obedient people to seek God and make Him the priority of their life. Zephaniah paints a picture of future salvation in which Judah and all the nations will come together to offer worship to the Lord. The book of Zephaniah ends on a positive note. God will bless Judah and all the nations of the world. In a very real sense Zephaniah is describing the end times when all issues between God and humankind will be resolved. There will be dancing and celebration in the streets.

Reflections and Comments

Complacency:

The people of Judah had developed a religious attitude that allowed them to ignore God in their lives. They had come to the belief that God was indifferent in regard to his people. God no longer mattered in the scheme of things. "Neither good nor evil can the Lord do." (Zephaniah 1:12) God was no longer relevant to a people whose hearts were stagnant and who were eager to do their evil deeds. Israel was a shameless nation. The nation that Zephaniah encountered was not unlike the society we experience today. There is corruption and greed; there is injustice; there is the disposal of unwanted children and there is every reason to believe that the "Day of the Lord" is coming. What we need are prophets willing to listen to the call of God and tell people just how disappointed God is with the world.

Return to the Lord:

The closing verse of Zephaniah summarizes the Lord's promises. Israel's future will be great if the Israelites return to the service of the Lord. Those promises extend to us. Serve the Lord in all that you do and God will reward you for your efforts. Zephaniah looked at his world and yet he was able to be optimistic in spite of all that he could see. Should we not be able to be optimistic as well? Praise the Lord! Trust in Him!

Promise and hope:

Zephaniah like the prophets that went before him warns the people of disaster ahead. You may think that God does not keep track of your deeds, but trust me he does. Those who do not believe in the Lord will suffer. Those who ignore and defy the Lord will be left with nothing of value. False gods do not have the power to help anyone. Your hope and your future lie with the Lord. Seek the Lord, obey his laws, be humble and the Lord will shelter you on the day of his anger. God's promise is clear, "I will remove from your midst the proud braggarts." (Zephaniah 3:11) Not only will the wicked be removed, but the Lord will leave a remnant in your midst. A people loyal and humble will be left to take refuge in the Lord. Be glad and rejoice with all your heart! Zephaniah's message is direct, profound and to the point, trust in the Lord and things will turn well.

Zephaniah

Chapter 1	**The "Day of the Lord" is coming**
1:1	Zephaniah is commissioned by God
1:2 – 4	Judgment is coming on Judah
1:5 – 6	Judgment on those who do not seek
1:7 – 13	Keep silent before the Lord
1:14 – 18	Near is the day of the Lord
Chapter 2	**A plea for repentance**
2:1 – 3	Return to the Lord
2:4 – 9	God will judge the nations
2:10 – 12	Their pride is their downfall
Chapter 3	**Reproach and promise**
3:1 – 5	Jerusalem ignores God
3:6	God will deal with the nations
3:7 – 10	Repent and return to the Lord
3:11 – 13	Do no wrong, speak no lies
3:14	Be glad and rejoice in the Lord
3:15 – 18	The Lord is in your midst
3:19 – 20	Rejoice in God's salvation

The New American Bible: pages 1024 – 1027
Copyright: Catholic Publishers, Inc. 1971
A Division of Thomas Nelson, Inc.

CHAPTER EIGHT

The Prophet
Jeremiah

Jeremiah

The eighth prophet in our study is Jeremiah. He is the second of the Major Prophets we have encountered thus far. There are four Major Prophets identified in the Catholic bible. In Jewish tradition Daniel is not numbered as one of the four and he is placed under Writings. The Hebrew Old Testament has a threefold division: the Torah, the Prophets, and the Writings. Jeremiah is known as the prophet to the nations. His prophetic activity extends some forty-five years in all. He begins his ministry in 627 during the reign of Josiah. He prophesied during the reigns of the last five kings of Judah. He does not disappear from sight until about 582. Jeremiah experienced the terrible siege and destruction of Jerusalem by Babylon in 587/586. While Jeremiah's main focus was Judah he lived through the Assyrian, Egyptian and Babylonian ascendancy, domination and decline. It was clear that he interacted with foreign nations who respected him as a prophet. Convinced of God's universal sovereignty he saw no national limits to his ministry. God was part of Jeremiah's life from the very beginning, "Before I formed you in the womb I dedicated you a prophet to the nations…". (Jeremiah 1:5) Jeremiah felt that he was not the one for the job. He told the Lord that he was too young and was not very good at making speeches. The Lord told Jeremiah not to worry as He the Lord would be with him. The Lord then extended his hand and placed His words into the mouth of Jeremiah. The book of Jeremiah is filled with images. In chapter 1 we have the almond tree and the boiling kettle. Because the almond tree begins to bloom in late winter it is called "the watcher". It signals the coming of spring. Jeremiah lets the people of Israel know that the Lord is watching them. Just as spring is coming they should know that God's word will be done. Punishment is coming. The boiling kettle is a symbol and a sign of an invasion coming from the north signaling the rise of the Assyrians. Jeremiah reminds the people that in the beginning of the relationship between God and His people there was so much promise of the good things to come. Unfortunately, the concerns of the world distracted them away for the service of their God. What could have been was lost in the fear and anxiety of daily living. All they had to do was remain faithful to the service of the Lord. Even after Judah saw what happened to Israel, they continued to ignore the Lord. Samaria, the capital city of Israel, was destroyed in 722 by Assyria. Jeremiah offered his temple sermon as a warning to the people that failure to listen to the word of God was not good. Moses in the book of Deuteronomy pointed out that behavior has consequences. Serve the Lord and good things will happen. In the book of Jeremiah, we find words that were applied to Jesus in the New Testament. "Yet I was like a trusting lamb led to slaughter, not knowing that they were hatching plots against me." (Jeremiah 11:19) "Like a sheep he was led to slaughter…". (Acts 8:32) From the beginning people tried to silence Jeremiah even to the point of threatening his life. The men in his hometown told him not to prophecy or they would kill him. Jeremiah tells his people that war, famine and disease are some of the ways that humans are given wake up calls. Their choices and their behavior inflicts harm on themselves and their neighbors. It does not have to be that way. The more Jeremiah pointed out just how unhappy God was with the world the more criticism he received. Frustration was a part of the life of each and every prophet God sent to remind the people just how far short they fell from pleasing their God. At one point Jeremiah complains, "I neither borrow nor lend yet everyone curses me." (Jeremiah 15:10) Throughout his ministry Jeremiah faced many challenges often his frustration was expressed openly. "All day long I am an object of laughter, everyone mocks me." (Jeremiah 20: 7) I think to myself I will no longer proclaim the death and destruction that is coming. God's message burns within my heart and I cannot resist, I must speak out, I must warn the house of Israel. They put me in prison for telling the truth. They do not want to hear what I have to say and yet they continue to ask me what does the Lord have to say? "Woe to the shepherds who destroy and scatter my flock." (Jeremiah 23:1) Jesus saw the vast crowd, "his heart was moved to pity for them, for they were like sheep without a shepherd;" (Mark 6:34). The leaders, the priests, the prophets and the kings failed the people of God. The people needed leadership and guidance and they were given arrogance and pride. Jeremiah looks beyond the fall of Jerusalem. God and Jeremiah will be vindicated. The people had been convinced that they had nothing to fear. God had protected Jerusalem from destruction once before. Surrounded by the Assyrians a plague broke out among the army of Sennacherib and he had to withdraw before he could destroy the city. If God would protect Jerusalem once would he not do so again? The people felt they were free to act without any fear of consequences. Jeremiah told Israel that Jerusalem would be destroyed for their arrogance and pride. Clearly this was a message the people and their leaders did not wish to hear. They attacked Jeremiah for having the courage to tell them the truth. "When Jeremiah finished speaking all that the Lord commanded him to speak to all the people, then the priests, the prophets, and all the people laid hold of him crying, 'You must die!' (Jeremiah 26:8) The elders spoke up saying this man does not deserve death for speaking the truth. Did not the prophet Micah do the same thing and he was not put to death? Jeremiah was spared on this occasion and yet he continued to be in hot water with the leaders, the prophets, the priests and the people. Chapters 30 to 33 deal with themes of hope, restoration and a new covenant. The Babylonians surrounded Jerusalem prior to destroying the city and ultimately the temple. The people believed that God would save them as he had done when the Assyrians had surrounded the city. Jeremiah warns them that God is not going to intervene and the temple will be destroyed. It is at this critical moment that the very people from his hometown that earlier had threaten to kill Jeremiah arrived in Jerusalem to ask Jeremiah if he wanted to buy one of his family fields as was his right under Jewish law. Jeremiah thought that buying a piece of property when the Babylonians were in control did not make a lot of sense. God told Jeremiah to go ahead and buy the land as his investment would be in good hands. Have confidence in the Lord! God will restore the land to the people, Jeremiah's purchase will be safe. God is always eager to show his people mercy and forgiveness. Jeremiah told the king of Judah that the king of Babylon would make him captive and send him to Babylon where he will have a peaceful death. The king did not appreciate what Jeremiah was telling him and he placed Jeremiah under house arrest and barred him from entering the temple. Jeremiah dictated God's words to his secretary who wrote them down on a scroll. Jeremiah told his secretary to take the scroll to the temple and read it to the people. Friends of the king seized the scroll and took it to the king that he might hear what God had told Jeremiah to tell the people. The king believing that if he destroyed that scroll what was written on it would not happen. As the scroll was being read to the king he had the scribe stop the reading ever three or four sentences and cut that part away from the scroll and thrown the piece into the fire. He did this until the entire scroll had been read, cut off piece by piece and the entire scroll had been consumed by the fire. The king wanted Jeremiah and his secretary arrested. God had told them to go into hiding. God asked Jeremiah to make a second scroll replacing the one that had been thrown into the fire. It was at this time Jeremiah decided to go to his hometown and look at the land he had purchased. The city Jerusalem had been surrounded and the enemy had left to deal with an Egyptian up rising. Jeremiah was leaving the city when the captain of the guard arrested Jeremiah. Jeremiah was accused of desertion in the face of the enemy, charged with treason and put into prison. They wanted to kill Jeremiah for saying that the people in Jerusalem will die either by the sword, disease or famine. Not wishing to kill a prophet by their hand they put him in a muddy cistern hoping that he would drown in the mud or die of starvation. He did neither as God rescued him by the hand of Ebed-melech the Ethiopian, a friend of Jeremiah and a court official. In the end the city was captured, the king blinded and sent into exile. The temple was destroyed and the consequences of failing to listen to the Lord and his prophets was realized. The story of Jeremiah ends in Egypt. The book of Jeremiah ends with the listing of God's punishment of the nations who had helped in the destruction of Jerusalem. Jeremiah was commissioned from the womb as a prophet to the nations. To understand Jeremiah's ministry, one must have some basic understanding of the turmoil, the political intrigue and the unstable nature of the Middle East. During the first three quarters of the seventh century, the Assyrian Empire flourished. It even conquered Egypt and for a time occupied it. Jeremiah saw the destruction of Samaria, the siege of Jerusalem, he witnessed the downfall of Assyria and the rise of Babylon. He was present when the temple in Jerusalem was demolished. It was a period that experienced five different kings of Judah, a number of assassinations, many plots and behind the scenes deals, shifting allegiances, intrigue and uncertainty for the future. Only Jeremiah knew what was going to happened and it was he that the leaders, the prophets, the priests and the people refused to listen to and in fact persecuted. Like many of the other prophets Jeremiah focused upon the failure of Judah to keep faith with the covenant. Jeremiah's indictments pointed out the sins of Judah. They were guilty of idolatry, social injustice and religious hypocrisy. Throughout the Book of Jeremiah, we are reminded that Jeremiah was engaged in serious conflict and dialogue with the political powers of Jerusalem, the king, the king's prophets, the leaders, the priests and the people on an almost daily basis. Jeremiah never stopped preaching against two major evils of his day: idolatry and injustice. He was relentless even when it led to great personal suffering and persecution. He often pleaded for his people to be converted and come back to God's covenant. When the people refused to listen to his words, Jeremiah felt the anguish personally. All he ever wanted for his people was that they return to the service of God. He wanted his people to receive the message of God's desire to forgive his people. God desired to show His tender loving mercy for Israel and Judah. Often the prophet would seem to be on the verge of despair over the evil that he saw all around him. He knew that it did not have to be this way. As Jeremiah predicted, the nation Judah, was eventually punished for their sin and disobedience. In 586 Jerusalem was destroyed and their leading citizens were led into exile in Babylon. Jeremiah's message was one that called his people to return to the service of the Lord. In 640, at the age of eight, Josiah became the king of Judah and began a resurgence of national and religious rebuilding. In 622 workers restoring the Temple found an ancient law book. The book became the basis of religious reform modelled after the Book of Deuteronomy. Unfortunately, the promising reform was cut short by Josiah's unexpected death.

Reflections and Comments

Typology:

The likeness of the Old Testament compared to the New Testament constitutes the application of the principles of biblical theology. A type can be defined as "a biblical person, event or institution that serves as an example for other persons, events or institutions." It is as simple as taking a person in the Old Testament and connecting that person with a person in the New Testament. Adam is an Old Testament person. Jesus is a New Testament person. Adam was responsible for breaking the relationship between God and man. Jesus was the one who restored the relationship between God and man. A person in the Old Testament foreshadows an event in the New Testament. "Typology was used in the preaching of the apostles as an argument to establish the truth of their message." (The Bible and the Liturgy: Jean Danielou page 5) What happens in the Old Testament finds fulfillment in the New Testament. Joseph, the son of Jacob was sold for twenty pieces of silver in the Old Testament. Jesus the Son of God was sold for thirty pieces of silver in the New Testament. Jeremiah in the Old Testament foreshadowed Jesus in the New Testament. Jeremiah wept over Jerusalem. Jesus wept over Jerusalem. A person in the Old Testament preforms an action which occurs in the New Testament. What is promised in the Old is fulfilled in the New. Most of the prophets described persons, events and institutions, which were contemporary to their understanding and yet carrying meaningful significance for the future. Moses crossing the Red Sea is symbolic of the waters of Baptism. The Israelites entered the water as slaves and emerge as free people. Christians enter the waters of Baptism with sin and emerge free of original sin. The New Testament identifies numerous Old Testament passages that are fulfilled typologically.

Covenant:

Early in Jeremiah's ministry, when Josiah at the age of eight came to the throne of Judah with the help of people eager for reform, Josiah initiated a resurgence of national and religious rebuilding. Further impetus was given to his reform when in 622, workers restoring the Temple found an ancient law book. The Book of Deuteronomy became the heart of the religious reform. (2Kings 22:1 – 23:27) The promised reform was cut short by Josiah's unexpected death. The Bible's imagery of covenant focuses upon the relationship between God and humankind. All of the prophets were familiar with the concept of covenant. The covenant with Adam and Eve, the covenant with Noah, the covenant with Abraham, the covenant with Moses, the Davidic covenant and the foreshadowing of the New Covenant are contained in the Bible. The writings of the prophets revolved around the faithlessness of the chosen nation and its failure to live up to its covenant obligations.

When does life begin:

"Before I formed you in the womb I knew you." (Jeremiah 1:5) Jeremiah was called to be a prophet while he was in the womb. For Jeremiah his life began at the moment of his conception. The Old Testament had no confusion about when life began. The same is true for the New Testament. "When Elizabeth heard Mary's greeting, the baby leapt in her womb." (Luke 1:41) John the Baptist acknowledged the presence of Jesus while he was in the womb. There are those who would have you believe that life begins at birth. If that were true what would be the point in harvesting a fetus, why not wait for the birth to harvest body parts. Today's society could learn a great deal from the Bible should they be willing to listen.

I am too young:

Jeremiah recognized the importance of God's call; yet he felt unworthy and he believed that someone else would likely be able to do a better job than he could. God told Jeremiah not to worry because God would be with him. God told Jeremiah not to get married as his job as prophet would be quite demanding. God told Jeremiah that the leaders, the priests, the prophets and the people would not listen to what he had to say. God told Jeremiah that his life would be filled with misunderstanding, pain and suffering. What people often fail to realize is that the prophets had a choice to do what God had asked or simply walk away from their responsibility. How often do people fail to do what is in their best self-interest? Even Jonah figured it out eventually. Let not the wise person take pride in knowledge, nor the strong person in strength, nor the rich in wealth, rather let them seek and find glory in the Lord.

Obey the Lord:

The world that Jeremiah confronted is not unlike the one we live in today. Jeremiah knew that God's patience was not without limit. He knew that the Middle East was unstable. He knew that people do not always behave in their best self-interest. He knew that turmoil was inevitable. What really hurt was he knew that it did not have to be this way.

Jeremiah

Chapter 1 to 6   **A broken covenant**

1:1 – 3   Oracles in the days of Josiah
1:4 – 9   The call of Jeremiah from the womb
1:10   Appointed a prophet to the nations
1:11 – 14   An almond tree and a boiling pot
1:15 – 19   Place your confidence in God
2:1 – 17   Promise and infidelity
2:18 – 29   Disobedience and rebellion
2:30 – 37   My people have forgotten me
3:1 – 5   A call to repentance
3:6 – 11   Lessons unlearned Judah and Israel
3:12 – 18   Israel admit your guilt
3:19 – 25   You have sinned against the Lord
4:1 – 4   Judgment is coming
4:5 – 31   The invasion from the north
5:1 – 6   Universal corruption
5:7 – 19   Why should God forgive you?
5:20 – 31   You have eyes but do not see
6:1 – 7   The enemy is at the gate
6:8 – 18   Be warned Jerusalem
6:19 – 30   God will bring evil upon this people

Chapter 7 to 10   **False religion punished**

7:1 – 15   Temple sermon

7:16 – 20	Abuses in worship
7:21 – 29	The people have not listened
7:30 – 34	Child sacrifice
8:1 – 3	A disgraced people
8:4 – 9	Israel's conduct incomprehensible
8:13 – 17	Threats of punishment
8:18 – 23	Jeremiah grieves over his people
9:1 – 8	A corrupt people
9:24	The uncircumcised at heart
10:1 – 5	The folly of idolatry
10:6 – 16	The Lord is great and powerful
10:17 – 22	Judah will be punished
10:23 – 25	A prayer of Jeremiah

Chapters 11 to 20   A warning of consequences

11:1 – 14	Remain faithful to the covenant
11:15 – 17	Israel and Judah have done evil
11:18 – 23	A plot against Jeremiah
12:1 – 6	Jeremiah wants God to act
12:7 – 13	The Lord's complaint
12:14 – 17	Judah's neighbor
13:1 – 11	The rotted loincloth lesson
13:12 – 15	The broken wine flask
13:16 – 17	A last warning
13:18 – 19	Judah will face exile
13:20 – 27	Woe to you Jerusalem!

14:1 – 10	The great drought punishment for sins
14:11 – 22	God alone can do all things
15:1 – 4	Punishment for the sins of Manasseh
15:5 – 9	The scene of tragedy
15:10 – 21	Jeremiah's complaint
16:1 – 13	God tells Jeremiah not to take a family
16:14 – 18	Their sins are not hidden from God
16:19 – 21	The conversion of the nations
17:1 – 4	God will plunder their wealth
17:5 – 11	True wisdom
17:12 – 18	Heal me, Lord
17:19 – 27	True wisdom is found in the Lord
18:1 – 12	The potter's vessel
18:13 – 17	Apostasy, Israel has forgotten the Lord
18:18 – 23	Come! Devise a plot against Jeremiah
19:1 – 9	The potter's house
19:10 – 14	The shattered clay pot
20:1 – 6	A discouraged Jeremiah
20:7 – 18	Jeremiah's interior crisis

Chapters 21 to 29   The final days

21:1 – 10	The fate of Zedekiah and Jerusalem
21:11 – 14	To the royal house of Judah
22:1 – 8	Listen to the word of the Lord
22:9 – 12	Weep for the king of Judah
22:13 – 19	Woe to the one guilty of wrongdoing

22:20 – 30	Woe to shepherds who do not listen
23:1 – 8	A just shepherd will gather his flock
23:9 – 40	False prophets
24:1 – 10	Two baskets of figs
25:1 – 13	Seventy years of exile
25:14 – 38	The cup of judgment
26:1 – 9	The temple sermon
26:10 – 15	Jeremiah threatened with death
26:16 – 19	The Micah defense
26:20 – 24	The fate of Uriah
27:1 – 22	Serve Babylon or perish
28:1 – 11	The two yokes
28:12 – 17	The false prophet Hananiah
29:1 – 23	A letter to the exiles in Babylon
29:24 – 32	The false prophet Shemaiah

Chapters 30 to 33 The restoration

30:1 – 6	Write down on a scroll
30:8 – 16	God will protect you
30:17 – 24	God will heal all your injuries
31:1 – 6	I will be your God
31:7 – 14	The Lord will save his people
31:15 – 20	You sorrow will turn to joy
31:21 – 30	A summons to return home
31:31 – 34	The new covenant
31:35 – 37	God is trustworthy
31:38 – 40	Jerusalem will be rebuilt

32:1 – 5	The Babylonians take Jerusalem
32:6 – 25	Who buys land during a siege?
32:26 – 35	The sins of Judah
32:36 – 44	A pledge of future restoration
33:1 – 11	A time of healing and peace
33:12 – 26	A promise of one to come

Chapters 34 to 45 The last days

34:1 – 7	The fate of Zedekiah
34:8 – 11	The pact broken
34:12 – 22	Your word is no good Judah
35:1 – 11	The faithful Rechabites
35:12 – 19	Reward for faithfulness
36:1 – 10	Baruch, the scribe of Jeremiah
36:11 – 26	The king's reaction to the scroll
36:27 – 31	Write a second scroll
37:1 – 10	Jeremiah in the dungeon
37:11 – 14	Jeremiah accused of desertion
37:15 – 21	Jeremiah beaten and imprisoned
38:1 – 6	Jeremiah in the muddy cistern
38:7-13	Ebed-melech to the rescue
38:14 – 28	The king seeks advice
39:1 – 10	The capture of Jerusalem
39:11 – 14	Jeremiah is released
39:15 – 18	Ebed-melech rewarded
40:1 – 12	Jeremiah given a choice
40:13 – 16	An assassination plot

41:1 – 10	Ishmael carries out his plan
41:11 – 18	The exodus in reverse
42:1 – 6	Jeremiah is consulted
42:7 – 18	Jeremiah advises the remnant
42:18 – 22	Do not go to Egypt
43:1 – 7	Jeremiah accused of lying
43:8 – 13	The fate of those in Egypt
44:1 – 6	Israel falls back into idolatry
44:7 – 14	You have not learned from the past
44:15 – 23	You continue to sin against the Lord
44:24 – 30	God's patience runs out
45:1 – 5	A message to Baruch

Chapters 46 to 51   Oracles against the nations

46:1 – 28	Against Egypt
47:1 – 7	Against the Philistines
48:1 – 47	Against Moab
49:1 – 6	Against the Ammonites
49:7 – 22	Against Edom
49:23 – 27	Against Damascus
49:28 – 33	Against Arabia
49:34 – 39	Against Elam
50:1 – 46	The first oracle against Babylon
51:1 – 58	The second oracle against Babylon
51:59 – 64	The prophecy sent to Babylon

Chapter 52	**Historical appendix**
52:1 – 11	The capture of Jerusalem
52:12 – 30	The destruction of Jerusalem
52:31 – 34	Favor shown to Jehoiachin

The Book of Lamentations	**Five poems of mourning**
	An anguished response to the destruction of Jerusalem 587 B.C.

The New American Bible: pages 841-900
Copyright: Catholic Publishers, Inc. 1971
A Division of Thomas Nelson, Inc.

PART TWO

THE TABLE OF CONTENTS

9. HABAKKUK......620 – 598 93

10. DANIEL.......... 606 – 534 101

11. OBADIAH.......588 – 583 110

12. EZEKIEL..........595 – 536 118

13. HAGGAI ....520 – 518 134

14. ZECHARIAH..520 – 518 141

15. JOEL .... 445 – 400 150

16. MALACHI......450 – 420 159

CHAPTER NINE

The Prophet Habakkuk

Habakkuk

Our ninth prophet is Habakkuk. His book contains no historical reference tying his prophecy to a specific time in history. As with the other prophets, we know very little about him. His text tells us that he lived at a time when Babylon was taking over the area from the fallen Assyrians. The prophecy of Habakkuk is considerably more reflective than that of Nahum. Habakkuk entertains the age old question of evil in the world. Living in a world saturated with godlessness and injustice, Habakkuk questions divine holiness and justice. Habakkuk was a contemporary of Jeremiah. The question that he asked is "why do the wicked prosper?" All of the prophets we have looked at thus far saw a world full of corruption, social injustice and religious hypocrisy. Another question that Habakkuk asked is "why does God allow evil to exist in the world?" The wisdom literature of the Old Testament considered this question. The answer is quite simple and straight foreword: God gave man a free will. We are able to select a false good. We choose things that are not good for us because we can. There will come a time when the weight of our poor choices will become so heavy that we will be unable to lift or deal with the consequences in our lives. It is usually at this point that we turn to God for help. God becomes our help of last resort. The prophets told the people, the leaders, the priests and the false prophets that God should be their help of first resort. Don't turn to God after you have tried everything you can think of to resolve the difficulty. Turn to God from the very beginning and He will take care of you. Habakkuk has a third question for God: "Why is God willing to use a nation more wicked than Judah to punish His people?" Babylon will become the instrument that will destroy Jerusalem and its Temple. Judah has its lack of faith, its measure of evil and its rebellious heart, but as evil as Judah is, they do not believe they are as evil as Babylon. To suggest that Israel with all its bad behavior is at least not as bad, not as evil as its neighbors, appears to be a rush to the bottom of the moral scale. To base morality upon the least one may achieve rather than the most one may accomplish, allows moral criterion to become relative rather than absolute. Beneath the surface of his prophecies lies an unexpressed narrative of Habakkuk's personal spiritual journey to resolve a number of religious issues. Trapped in a sinful society, he wonders why God does not do something in the face of such prevailing corruption? Why does God allow evil to exit? It is beyond Habakkuk's knowledge and understanding. There are those who would suggest that God knows what life will be like for the wicked in the next world and he allows the wicked to enjoy life now, because He knows that it will not be pleasant later. The parable of the rich man and Lazarus is the case in point. The rich man had an easy life here on earth. The poor man, Lazarus had a difficult life here on earth. Both men eventually died and their situations change. Luke 16:25 "My child, replied Abraham, remember that you were well off in your lifetime, while Lazarus was in misery. Now he has found consolation here, but you have found torment. And that is not all. Between you and us there is fixed a great abyss..." neither of us may cross. The lesson to be learned is that God is in charge, even though justice is not always apparent in this world one must trust in the Lord and be patient. Habakkuk, driven to prayer, saw God's justice in action in the past. God freed Israel from its oppressors. God led his chosen people out of Egypt to the promise land. Habakkuk is convinced that his spiritual journey is concluded. He will trust in the Lord, come what may. He has learned that no matter how difficult life may become, the only logical course of action is to trust in the Lord. None of us has all the answers. We are called to live a life of faith. Habakkuk concludes his book with the following statement: "Yet will I rejoice in the Lord and exult in my saving God. God, my Lord, is my strength; he makes my feet swift as those of hinds and enables me to go upon the heights." (Habakkuk 3:18) Trust in the Lord! Habakkuk prophesied when Babylon was in the process of replacing Assyria in the Near East as the power in the region. Habakkuk was concerned with the amount of social injustice that existed in Jewish society. Jeremiah had complained about the king of Judah, the oppression and the exploitation apparent in Jewish society and the religious hypocrisy evident at all levels. Habakkuk saw exactly the same things that had irritated Jeremiah. While Habakkuk's basic message is similar to that of the other prophets the style of his book is unique. Its literary style is similar to that of the Wisdom books and the Psalms. Habakkuk makes an important and original contribution to the sum of Israel's reflection on the nature of its God and how God deals with His chosen people. The book begins with a question which the prophet dares to address to God. Why does God allow evil to exist in the world? A second inquiry is implied in the discussion the prophet has with God. Does God really care about His people? Despite the concerns expressed there is an underlying attitude of faith and trust. In chapter three of his book Habakkuk affirms that God is sovereign and in control of history. Habakkuk's final thoughts are upbeat. Trust in the Lord! Be patient! Rejoice, God is in charge! He who trusts in the Word of God may suffer and bemoan his state in life for a little while, but in the end if he perseveres in being faithful to the Lord, he will rejoice. Habakkuk was inspired by God to deliver a message that condemned evil and yet asked the people to trust in God's saving power. God's plan must be carried out. He will punish his own people for their evil behavior and he will punish Babylon. God tells Habakkuk not to be impatient. Sometimes we look for immediate results and we grow impatient when things do not happen as quickly as we would like. The lesson is clear. It is based on the conviction that God is just and so justice must ultimately prevail. The only question is "how long?" It is a question that has been asked in every generation. The final answer lies in the future. Faith does not depend on the fulfillment of its expectations, but on its power to transform lives. The faith of Habakkuk finds its most poetic expression in chapter 3. What the prophet envisages is a decisive intervention of God to wipe out all wickedness and oppression. Habakkuk realizes that it is just a matter of time. In the struggle of good and evil Habakkuk declares God the winner.

Reflections and Comments

God's Ways:

It should come as no surprise that Habakkuk's idea of justice was different from God's idea of justice. If it were up to Habakkuk, he would simply destroy all that were evil in the world, beginning with the Babylonians and ending up with the leaders of Judah. The lesson that God teaches Habakkuk is the same lesson God taught Job. It is God who is in charge. He and He alone is sovereign. Habakkuk and Job arrive at the same conclusion, God is in charge and He does not need our help. Certainly there are times when we ask the same question. Why does God allow evil to exist? Be still and know that I am your God and you are my people! Often the most difficult advice to follow is the simplest offered. When we see something that we feel is wrong, our inclination is to fix it. It has been suggested that the first stages of eternal life will be spent thanking God for not answering most of our prayers.

Why:

The question Habakkuk asked is one that the wisdom writings attempted to answer. Why does God allow evil to exist? Clearly God could see how corrupt Judah had become. Why would God use Babylon to punish Judah? Evil made no sense to Habakkuk and even today the world has not improved in its efforts to eliminate pain and suffering from the lives of people. There are millions of people that are homeless, without hope and desperate to make their lives have some meaning. It is interesting to note that God did not become angry with the impatience displayed by Habakkuk. God could have said that he did destroy all evil in the world once before with the big flood. Evil, like an unwanted cancer, returned with a vengeance. God promised not to destroy the world again. Habakkuk's perplexity ultimately gave way to a simple act of trust in God based upon the realization God is in charge. Peace and justice come from God. God is not bound by time and place. God's ways are not our ways. The Book of Habakkuk assures us that God, in His own time, will bring justice to the world and will triumph over the wicked and will deliver the faithful. "Though the flocks disappear from the fold and there be no herd in the stalls, yet will I rejoice in the Lord and exult in my saving God. God, my Lord, is my strength; he makes my feet swift as those of hinds and enables me to go upon the heights." (Habakkuk 3:18)

Habakkuk

Chapter 1	**A question of God's justice**
1:1	What the prophet received in a vision
1:2 – 4	Habakkuk's first complaint
1:5 – 11	God's response
1:12 – 17	Habakkuk's second complaint
Chapter 2	**A dialogue with God**
2:1 – 2	I will wait for God's answer
2:2 – 4	God's response
2:5 – 13	Sayings against Tyrants
2:14 – 20	The knowledge of God's glory
Chapter 3	**A hymn about God's reign**
3:1 – 16	Rejoice in the Lord
3:17 – 19	Though the fig tree does not blossom

The New American Bible: pages 1020 – 1023
Copyright: Catholic Publishers, Inc. 1971
A Division of Thomas Nelson, Inc.

CHAPTER TEN

The Prophet
Daniel

Daniel

The book of Daniel was written primarily for the purpose of encouraging the Jewish nation to remain faithful to their God. The allurements of Babylonian paganism coupled with the endless number of years of exile had begun to have its effect on the people. As we have seen, Moses in the book of Deuteronomy had warned the people about imitating the behavior of one's neighbor. Daniel was concerned with demonstrating the superior wisdom of Israel's God over the human wisdom of the pagans. He detailed the advantage of trusting in God in a series of six edifying stories about Daniel and his three companions. Daniel's message is of enduring worth to all generations. His story is meant not only for believers of his own age and place, but for all times. God is the master of history, who uses the rise and fall of nations as necessary steps in the establishment of his universal reign over all peoples. The book of Daniel is not overly concerned with historical accuracy. The opening stories are a means of conveying a religious message, like the parables of Jesus. The stories give a degree of insight into the life of Jewish exiles in Babylon. Daniel was taken into exile as a teenager in 605 B.C. The Book of Daniel is divided into three parts. Part one consists of six stories concerning Daniel and his three companions at the royal court in Babylon. Part two contains four visions and are revelations characterized as apocalyptic literature. Part three is a set of three additional stories of Daniel's exploits found only in the Catholic bible. The Book of Daniel clearly states that a person of faith can resist temptation and conquer adversity. The Lord will never abandon a person of faith. It is possible for a Christian to live in a godless society, set an example of faithfulness and never shy away from affirming the faith. The first story is the food test. The second is the composite statue. The third is the fiery furnace. The fourth is the dream of the great tree. The fifth is the writing on the wall. The sixth and last story is Daniel in the lion's den. The Jews in exile needed encouragement and that is exactly what the Book of Daniel provided. These stories express confidence that the truth of Jewish religion is powerful enough to impress any person of good will. By the same token, any Christian who lives their life in a faithful manner offers to the world an example of the true love that motivates their behavior. As in the time of Daniel, so in the time of Jesus we live by faith in the midst of a godless world. Daniel's point is that the Jew and the Christian evangelize by example and indeed, actions do speak louder than words. The message of the Book of Daniel is unmistakable: God is sovereign and rules over all people and all kingdoms even though it does not always look that way. The Book of Daniel is filled with symbols and visions relating to events past and future. We will leave their interpretation to more qualified scholars and focus upon the underlying message. Daniel insists upon right conduct, solid faith, divine control over events and the certainty that the kingdom of God will ultimately triumph in the struggle of good and evil. The Book of Daniel exemplifies one possible way in which a faithful Jew or Christian may respond to a situation of oppression and persecution. Whether it is the right way can only be decided in the light of the specific circumstances of each situation, but it always demands serious consideration. "Apocalypse" is simply the Greek word for revelation. It denotes a certain kind of literature and a particular attitude with certain recurring characteristics. Authorship is often vague or tied to a famous person of the past. There is the presence of a mediating angel, a heavenly entity which explains the symbolism contained in the writing. The typical subject matter may contain predictions of the future, especially of a final judgment. This kind of writing was very popular from the third century B.C. on and in early Christian literature. Daniel 13 and 14 are three independent stories in which Daniel plays the center role. These short stories are excluded from the Jewish canon of Scripture. The Book of Daniel, strictly speaking, does not belong to the prophetic writings but rather to a distinctive type of literature known as "apocalyptic". This kind of writing appeared during times of persecution. It was meant to be a source of comfort and encouragement to people undergoing the ordeal of persecution and exile. The Jewish people were being forced to adopt foreign ways, including religious practices not in keeping with their traditions and practices. Daniel stood as an example of one who could resist the pressure to convert to Babylonian ways while remaining faithful to the God of Israel. The Book of Daniel insists upon right conduct, divine control over events, certainty that the kingdom of God will ultimately triumph and that humanity will reach the goal intended for it at the beginning of creation. Daniel answers the question of whether one who is committed to be faithful to God is able to live in a godless world. His answer is "yes"! God will never abandon those who trust and are faithful to Him. Most evangelical scholars conclude that the book of Daniel is historical and that the prophecies come from the sixth century B.C. The Catholic tradition along with a few evangelicals place the book in the second century B.C. It was seen to be composed during the bitter persecution carried on by Antiochus IV Epiphanes in (167 – 164 B.C.) The central message of Daniel is unmistakable. God is sovereign. He cannot be manipulated. God is in charge of history and He will bring all things to their proper end. In spite of how things might appear, God is in charge and all situations will be resolved as God desires. The book of Daniel begins with the explanation of how Daniel and his companions were carried off to Babylon. They remained faithful to their principles and passed every test they were given. They were true to God when other Jewish captives compromised their values. The book of Daniel is more than a treasure of prophetic literature. It paints a beautiful picture of a man of God who lived out his commitment in very troubled times. Daniel was able to remain true to the God of Israel even during very difficult times. The lesson is clear: people of faith can resist temptation and conquer any adversity. The second part of the book of Daniel, Chapters 7 to 12, contain imagery quite different from ones normally used by other prophets. All prophetic literature uses images, figures of speech and poetic language characterized by visionary symbolism, and yet the book of Daniel is unique in its use of apocalyptic symbolism. Chapters 13 and 14 are independent stories in which Daniel plays a part. They are not part of the Jewish or Christian Bible.

Reflections and Comments

Apocalyptic literature:

The Greek word "Apocalypse" means revelation. The word has come to be associated with a particular kind of revelation with a number of recurring characteristics. "Hopelessness" is one of the elements. Evil is intensifying and conditions are getting worse. The world is being attacked and trampled by wickedness. "God's sovereignty" is affirmed. The Lord can be trusted no matter how bad things appear. Heaven and earth may be destroyed, but God's words will never pass away. "Catastrophic judgment" is referenced. Something really bad is on the horizon and is about to happen. "Mediating angels" are present. The presence of angels emphasizes the supernatural character of the experience and adds to the sense of mystery. "Faithfulness" is valued. The one who stands firm to the end will be saved. The message of the visions is that pagan rulers are evil and in rebellion against God, but they will be defeated by the power of God.

Dreams and Visions:

Dreams are seen as the voice of God at night, while visions are usually daytime events. Daniel excelled in understanding and interpreting these events to the satisfaction of the kings of Babylon. God breaks into human experience through both dreams and visions. Some dreams are so obscure that a skilled wise man such as Daniel is required to render them intelligible. Nebuchadnezzar's dream falls into that category. The frequency and significance of dreams and visions stems from their importance as divine revelation to a particular individual. Apocalyptic imagery is inherently symbolic. It uses specific images to stand for something or someone else. Daniel's vision of a statue composed of various minerals is a symbolic picture of various empires. It is easy to get side tracked and caught up in explanations of past and future events. The point of the Book of Daniel is that four young Jewish men are able to remain faithful to their religious practices under circumstances that are less than ideal. All four were willing to put their lives on the line to remain faithful to the God of Israel. They lived their faith regardless of the cost, up to and including forfciting their lives if necessary to remain loyal to their God. Let others speculate whether Daniel's dreams and visions list catastrophes that precede a final judgment. These young men were and are living examples of the saying "be true to what you believe and it is not possible to deceive anyone". The gift of faith is the greatest gift a person can receive.

Daniel

Chapter 1 to 6 **Daniel and the kings of Babylon**

1:1 – 7	Daniel in exile: the food test
1:8 – 16	An opening story about diet
1:17 – 21	Reward for faithfulness
2:1 – 13	Nebuchadnezzar's dream
2:14 – 23	Daniel discovers its meaning
2:24 – 45	The mystery revealed
2:46 – 49	The king rewards Daniel
3:1 – 12	The fiery furnace
3:13 – 23	Shadrach, Meshach and Abednego
3:24 – 45	The prayer of Azariah
3:46 – 51	Stoking the fire
3:52 – 90	The prayer of the three
3:91 – 100	Deliverance from the furnace
4:1 – 14	Nebuchadnezzar's dream
4:15 – 24	Daniel's explanation
4:25 – 30	Nebuchadnezzar's madness
4:31 – 34	Nebuchadnezzar's return to health
5:1 – 12	The writing on the wall
5:13 – 16	The promise of gifts
5:17 – 30	The dream explained
6:1 – 9	Jealousy of Daniel's success
6: 10 – 19	Accusation and punishment of Daniel
6:20 – 24	Daniel's deliverance
6:25 – 29	Darius's decree

Chapter 7 to 12   Daniel's visions

7:1 – 10   The beasts and the judgment
7:11 – 14   One like the son of man
7:15 – 28   The interpretation
8:1 – 14   The ram and the he-goat
8:15 – 26   The angel Gabriel explains
8:27   The impact upon Daniel
9:1 – 2   Daniel refers to Jeremiah
9:3 – 19   Turning to God with prayer
9:20 – 27   Gabriel returns with an answer
10:1 – 9   An angelic vision
10:10 – 21   God has heard my prayer
11:1 – 20   Alexander the Great
11:21 – 45   Antiochus Epiphanes: the final conflict
12:1 – 4   The resurrection
12:5 – 13   The good will triumph

Chapter 13 to 14   Appendix

13:1 – 64   Susanna's virtue
14:1 – 42   Bel and the dragon

The New American Bible: pages 961 – 980
Copyright: Catholic Publishers, Inc. 1971
A Division of Thomas Nelson, Inc.

CHAPTER ELEVEN

The Prophet
Obadiah

Obadiah

Our eleventh prophet is Obadiah. He lived during a time of hardship, testing and suffering for Jerusalem. His book is the shortest book of the Old Testament, only twenty-one verses. As with other prophets we know very little about the prophet Obadiah. He prophesied against Edom reminiscent of Jonah and Nahum who condemned Nineveh, prior to its destruction. Obadiah's words against Edom occurred shortly after the fall of Jerusalem to the Babylonians in 586 B.C. Edom had acted as a good friend and neighbor of Judah off and on over the years. Their relationship would have been described as hot and cold depending upon the advantage to be gained by Edom. When it became obvious that the Babylonians would be victorious in destroying Jerusalem they joined in the plundering of Judah. Jeremiah 49 and Obadiah 1 share identical sentiments regarding the fate of Edom. God will deal with Edom predicting that just as Edom had turned its back on its brother Jacob so will their neighbors and their so called friends forsake them in their time of need. Obadiah points out that Edom's hostile actions against Jerusalem were particularly reprehensible because that nation was descended from Esau, Jacob's brother. The Edomite's lived in an area of the Black Sea. It was a harsh land and the very name "Edom" {which means, "red land"} describes their poor sandy soil unfit for farming. When the Babylonian armies captured Jerusalem, the king of Edom took advantage of the situation to seize large parts of the southern area of Judah. They applauded and took part in the sacking of Jerusalem. The ancestral kinship between Israel and Edom went all the way back to the conflict between Isaac's sons Esau and Jacob. Esau was a skilled hunter, a man of the field, preferred by his father and the first born of the two sons. He is portrayed in the Bible as a callous unrefined individual with moral and spiritual insensitivity. In the story of the exchanged birthright, Esau is a slave to his appetite, unable to delay immediate gratification for the sake of future benefit. He sold his birthright to Jacob for food. These events are detailed in Genesis 27. Jacob's deception occurred when Isaac was so old that his eyesight had failed. As the first born son, Esau was entitled to receive his father's blessing. The book of Genesis describes how Jacob and his mother obtained the father's blessing under false pretenses. Isaac believed that he was blessing Esau. The images associated with Esau are not all negative. Esau engenders feelings of pity and sorrow when we take into account the fact that he was a victim of deceit. A reader's sympathy aches for Esau when, upon his discovery of what Jacob had done, he cries and pleads with his father Isaac to give him a blessing. Esau was rejected and he was given no chance to receive the desired blessing. Later in Genesis 33 Jacob and Esau reconcile. To this day we have a proverb about selling one's birthright for the taste of food. Genesis 25:31 "But Jacob replied, 'First give me your birthright' in exchange for it. 'Look' said Esau, 'I'm on the point of dying. What good will any birthright do me?' But Jacob insisted, 'Swear to me first!' So Esau sold Jacob his birthright under oath." Obadiah is not the only prophet to speak unkindly against Edom. The list includes Amos, Jeremiah and Ezekiel. Edom's vengeful conduct is chronicled in their writings. The Book of Obadiah is basically a condemnation of Edom. No words of comfort or hope appear. There is a pledge that Edom will be destroyed. Edom had believed that it was secure from attack due to the fact that they lived in the mountains and access was at the very least difficult. Edom had strong fortresses securely located within a rugged mountain range. "You who live in the clefts of the rocks, who occupy the heights of the hill." (Jeremiah 49:16) The Edomite's controlled about seventy miles of the north-south trade route on the King's Highway between Ezion-geber and Damascus. The Edomite's profited from the tax they collected along the land ports built for that purpose. They even obstructed the migrating Israelites as they sought to traverse the King's Highway during the wilderness wanderings. (Numbers 20:14 – 21) Edom appears to represent all nations who take advantage of their neighbors. Obadiah contrasts the complete end of Edom with the people of Israel, who will not only survive, but will actually flourish and rule over the mountains of Edom. Israel's vindication is ultimately the vindication of God's sovereignty over all the nations. God's justice will be served. Edom, a nation known from early times for its wisdom was the home of Job and his friend Eliphaz. Obadiah was familiar with Edom's wisdom tradition and he could not figure out what God was thinking. He just knew that Edom had to be punished for their behavior. They had failed to show compassion in the day of their brother's trial and distress. God desires to save everyone and he asks that we treat each other with kindness and respect. Obadiah was a prophet of Judah. As with many of the Minor Prophets we know next to nothing about this author. Although the Edomite's obstructed the migrating Israelites during the wilderness wanderings the two neighbors seem to have lived peacefully until the reign of Saul. David's reign was marked by conflict with Edom. He defeated them in the Valley of the Salt. Their on-again-off-again relationship was reminiscent of Esau and Jacob's interaction of days past. Israel's hatred of Edom had deep roots. There were other prophets who held Edom accountable for their actions. Amos 1:11 – 12; Isaiah 21:11 – 12; Jeremiah 49:7 – 22; and Ezekiel 25:12 – 14. In the end all nations are accountable to God. Obadiah focuses his attention upon God's sense of justice against the wrongs committed by foreign nations. He points out in particular the wrongs of Edom finding pleasure in the troubles of Jerusalem. One of the lessons found in the Book of Genesis is that every time humans believe that God needs their help they manage to make things worse. Adam and Eve is a case in point. Abraham tried to help by having a child Ishmael, from the slave girl, Hagar. God gave Abraham a son, Isaac. Isaac had two sons Esau and Jacob. Some of the bitterest conflicts in history have occurred within families. Cain and Abel; Esau and Jacob down to the Hatfield's and the McCoy's. God does not need our help. What the prophets make clear is that humans must listen to God's word and obey His requests. Obadiah gets right to the point, God is not happy with Israel's neighbors and in particular with Edom. There is no escaping the Lord. The fact that Edomite's live in the mountains made them believe that they could not be touched, they were safe. God demonstrated that they could and they were overcome. The lesson for Edom is that the justice of the Lord will hold all nations accountable for what they have done. Edom will be held accountable for gloating over their brother's misfortune. Amen.

Reflections and Comments

Figures of speech:

The prophets convey their messages using a variety of colorful images. Their ability to express the word of God using fascinating combinations of wordplay, poetry, graphic figures of speech and other literary devices reveal sensitive, honest stewards who are faithful to the task that they were given. Analogy uses inference to suggest that certain resemblances imply further similarities may exist between two distinct items under discussion. The prophets use figures of speech to convey their messages in a colorful and distinct manner. To be "as quiet as a mouse" or "as annoying as finger nails on a chalkboard" are two examples. One of the more perplexing figures of speech is "anthropomorphism." The attribution of human features and behavior to nonhuman beings is common in both religious and profane literatures of all cultures. This type of figurative language is employed throughout the Old Testament. Thus God is described as having arms and legs, ears and feet etc. He walks and talks, gets angry, and becomes frustrated etc. Anthropomorphism allows us to discuss God in ways not otherwise available. The risk of humanizing God is accepted in order that the danger of thinking of Him as an abstraction or an impersonal force may be avoided. The Old Testament prophets do not write philosophical essays or theological treatises. They paint colorful pictures of a personal God.

The justice of God:

One of the themes of the prophets is their emphasis upon social and moral teaching. Over and over the prophets stressed that how we treat one another does matter. The poor person was not regarded as undesirable just because he or she was poor. It was the evil of others that had created this situation. Poverty and unjust oppression are frequent companions. The prophets were the people's conscience. They called attention to the disconnect between being the chosen covenant people and their behavior which reflected a commitment to follow their neighbors even to the point of worshipping false gods. Israel had largely abandoned its ancient ideals, assimilating itself to Gentile ways. It was the task of the prophets to remind the leaders, the priests, the false prophets and the people just how far they had wandered from the service of the God of Israel. Clearly, God's ways are not our ways. The justice of God requires that we show compassion in the day of our brothers and sisters distress. The corporal works of mercy stressed by Matthew (25:31 – 46) were more than ideals to be found in the life of every Christian. They were concrete proof that Our Lord's mission was alive and well living in the twenty-first century.

Obadiah

Chapter 1   **Obadiah's vision**

1:1   Title and Theme
1:2 – 5   Your pride will be your downfall
1:6 – 9   Your warriors shall be crushed
1:10 – 12   Your behavior is the reason
1:13 – 14   You showed no compassion

Judgment upon the Nations

1:15 – 16   The day of the Lord is near

Judah shall be restored

1:17 – 18   A remnant will survive
1:19   Edom will fall
1:20   Israel will occupy the land
1:21   The Lord will triumph

The New American Bible: pages 1005 – 1006
Copyright: Catholic Publishers, Inc. 1971
A Division of Thomas Nelson, Inc.

CHAPTER TWELVE

The Prophet
Ezekiel

Ezekiel

Our twelfth prophet is Ezekiel. Ezekiel was taken into captivity in 597 B.C. His primary audience was the Hebrew exiles in Babylon. His major emphasis stresses the sovereignty and glory of God and God's presence among the chosen people. Ten years prior to the destruction of Jerusalem, Ezekiel finds himself in Babylon. He was called to be a prophet in 593 B.C. Of note is the fact that God appeared to Ezekiel while he was in exile by a river in Babylon. The prophet Isaiah's encounter with God came while he was in the temple. God's presence was associated with the temple. With Ezekiel God's appearance took place in Babylon. God is not required to stay in one location. God is sovereign and He is free to appear to whomever He desires whenever He deems it appropriate and where ever He wishes. In the New Testament, access to God is granted everyone in every place. The curtain of separation is done away with for all time. Chapter 1 describes Ezekiel's call to be a prophet. His encounter with God is reminiscent of Isaiah's description of his encounter with God. (Isaiah 6) Ezekiel describes four living creatures and focuses attention upon the glory and holiness of God. God tells Ezekiel that the people are rebellious and probably won't listen to him. God's message must be proclaimed. God gives the people the opportunity to acknowledge their sins and repent. The Book of Ezekiel may be divided into three parts. Part one, chapters 1 to 24, emphasizes the judgment and destruction of Jerusalem. Part two, chapters 25 to 32, contains statements of judgment against the nations. Part three, chapters 33 to 48, looks to the future and the restoration of the nation of Israel. Symbolic actions reveal the true reality behind God's action. God gives Ezekiel a scroll to eat, demonstrating that the words of God reside in the person of Ezekiel and that the people should listen to what Ezekiel has to say. It is Ezekiel's mission to call the people to repentance. Chapters 4 to 7 contain object lessons and moral judgments. Ezekiel highlights Israel's sin of idolatry and the resulting judgment arising from their actions. He uses symbolic actions to focus attention upon future events; i.e. the siege map and lying on his side. An attacking army would build a wall around a city so that no help could reach the defenders nor survivors escape. The prophet is to lie on his left side, tied up and staring at his model the city of Jerusalem. The eating of unclean bread: i.e. this action is to bring out the desperation brought on by famine. The people will suffer greatly at the hands of their destroyers. The cutting off of the hair: i.e. by using a sword, which makes an unlikely razor, the prophet links haircutting to killing in battle. Since hair was a sign of strength; e.g., for Samson to be shaved bald was complete humiliation. The people will not be able to avoid the three evils of war: the burning of the city, death by the sword and exile. Ezekiel states clearly that the behavior of the chosen people has caused these events. They have no one to blame but themselves. The events in Ezekiel 8 to 10 take place five years prior to the fall of Jerusalem. God takes Ezekiel in a vision to the temple of Jerusalem to show him just how bad things have gotten. At the entrance to the north gate there is a pagan idol near the altar. All over the walls of the temple there are pagan images of unclean, detestable animals and seventy of Israel's elders are burning incense to these idols inside the temple. In the entrance to the north gate, woman were engaged in the ritualistic ceremony to a Mesopotamian god. Last but not least, twenty-five men are bowing down to a sun god with their backs to the temple. In the Ancient Near East, turning one's back toward his king or his god was an insult. These four events highlight just how bad the idolatry had become in Jerusalem. The sins of Judah became so horrific that the presence and holiness of God could no longer remain in the temple. In Ezekiel's vision, the presence of God moves from the inner Holy of Holies to the temple's threshold in preparation for leaving. In chapter 10, verse 18, God's glory leaves Jerusalem: "Then the glory of the Lord left the threshold of the temple…". Ezekiel encountered the same kind of false prophets that Jeremiah had to deal with in his time. Both prophets use the unfaithful wife/harlot imagery. Chapter 17 presents some historical information and background in the form of two eagles and a vine. When Babylon lay siege to Jerusalem, the king of Babylon, Nebuchadnezzar, took the king of Judah, Jehoiachin, into captivity in 597 B.C. and placed Jehoiachin's uncle Zedekiah as king in his place. Zedekiah entered into a solemn covenant treaty with Nebuchadnezzar. The first eagle represents the king of Babylon, Nebuchadnezzar and the second eagle represents Psammetichus II of Egypt. Zedekiah entered into a treaty with Egypt. He violated his covenant agreement with Nebuchadnezzar thus breaking his word. Ezekiel, God's prophet, points out that breaking a covenant or violating an oath taken with God as a witness, is a serious transgression of the second commandant; an action punishable by the judgment of God. Ezekiel uses the analogy of two eagles to pronounce judgment on King Zedekiah. God is serious about keeping one's word. The theme of individual responsibility and accountability plays an important role in Ezekiel's thinking. In chapter 18, Ezekiel quotes a popular proverb, "Fathers have eaten green grapes, thus their children's teeth are on edge"? The people use this concept to suggest that the sins of one's ancestors are visited upon their descendants. The children must pay for the sins of their parents. Ezekiel tells the people that this is not the case. Each individual will be judged by the merits of their actions. Ezekiel lists the terrible sins of Jerusalem and her leaders. They are guilty of killing innocent people, idolatry, social injustice, i.e., oppressing foreigners, widows and orphans; sexual misconduct, economic injustice and wishy-washy leadership. Included in the indictment are kings and nobility, priests, officials, prophets and the people. Ezekiel concludes part one with the words, "and they will know that I am God" (24:27). Part two, Chapters 25 to 32, contains judgment statements directed at Judah's seven hostile neighbors. God issues judgment against Ammon, Moab, Edom, Philistia, Sidon, Tyre and Egypt. God not only holds Judah and Samaria accountable for their behavior but all the nations are to be held accountable for their treatment of others. It is important how we treat others and everyone will stand before God to be judged; believers and non-believers alike. God is God of the universe. In part three, 33 to 48, Ezekiel, after the fall of Jerusalem, offers future hope and restoration. Because Israel and Judah rebelled against God and broke the Covenant, His presence left the Temple and the city of Jerusalem was destroyed. New life and restoration become the focus of Ezekiel's message. In chapter 37 we encounter the vision of the dry bones: A vision of a dead Israel restored to full life. The final symbolic action in the book has the prophet join two sticks together to form one staff. They represent the northern and the southern kingdoms as in the days of David and Solomon. If God can breathe life into dry bones he certainly is able to unify a people and restore that which was lost. The final chapters, 40 to 48, describe a New Covenant, a New Temple, a New Presence, a New Testament and a New Beginning. The prophets recognized just how important God's presence was to the Old Testament people. Encountered in the desert, carried into the promised land, placed in the temple, devastated when God left the temple before its destruction, Ezekiel saw a day when a new covenant, a new temple, a new beginning, would come to life in Jesus. A New Testament people would have direct access to God throughout the entire world. Wherever there is a tabernacle, that is where God is to be found. Scholars have differing views of Ezekiel 40 to 48, from a literal interpretation to a symbolic understanding, and thus fulfilled primarily in Christ (the new temple) and yet perhaps also pointing to the heavenly city in the Book of Revelations chapter 21 to chapter 22. Ezekiel is a remarkable individual; he is the fourth of the Major Prophets. He identifies himself as a priest and prophet. He was taken into exile in 597 and called by God in 593 to be a prophet to those Hebrew exiles in Babylon. In the opening verses of his book, Ezekiel tells us his location; "I was among the exiles by the river Chebar" (Ezekiel 1:1). He is described by scholars as favoring an older style of prophetic behavior which included dreams, trances, ecstasy and visions. He communicated with his fellow exiles using oral communication, symbolic actions, visions and prophetic discourse. His clear aim was to bring Israel to the knowledge of their sins committed against the Lord. Ezekiel sought to restore to prophecy some trust and some direction for his fellow exiles. He had received a vision of God's holiness and terrible power. His mission was not an easy one as he had to face a nation who were "rebellious and stubborn of heart", failing to listen or even hear the voice of God. Ezekiel did not have a choice as he saw it; he felt he must speak the words of the Lord whether anyone listened or not. Ezekiel is the prophet of hope. He preached individual responsibility, accountability for actions taken, God's holiness and sovereignty and that nothing is impossible where God is concerned. Put your trust in the Lord! Ezekiel was the first prophet to preach to a people who had neither a land nor a temple to call their own. Their temple had been destroyed and they had been taken from their own land. He stressed two important themes in his writings; the first was the sovereignty and glory of God. The Israelites may be in exile, but God was still in control of history. The second major theme was the presence of God. God was present with Moses, he was with the Israelites when they came out of Egypt and he took up residence in the Temple built by Solomon. He was forced to leave their presence because their sins drove him out of the Temple, and they were taken from their promised land. Ezekiel, as the prophet of hope, described a time when a glorious deliverance and a future restoration would take place, a new Temple and a new Covenant would come to light and the words of God will be remembered; "I will be your God and you will be my people". Ezekiel contrasts Israel's sinfulness with God's holiness and the fact that God will never completely abandon his people no matter how stubborn and stiff-necked they behave. The same may be said today; God will not abandon his people. Trust in the Lord and know that he will never abandon his chosen people.

Reflections and Comments

Individual Responsibility:

Each generation will be held responsible for its decisions. Now is the time to stand up and be counted. If there is to be any hope for the future, it requires a combination of faith and trust in God. The world that Ezekiel encountered is not unlike the world we live in today. There was an unwillingness to confront evil in all its forms. There was a reluctance to say or do anything that could be taken as an offense to hurt another's feelings. Ezekiel clearly understood that the root of Israel's problems lay in a gradual turning away from God and an embracing of the values of the world. The loss of knowing God is reflected in a willingness to redefine just who is in charge of worldly events. Mankind refuses to accept any responsibility for actions taken and is most willing to blame God for everything that goes wrong. God has become a scapegoat for the irresponsible.

Sin and Grace:

Ezekiel clearly took sin seriously. He recognized in the human heart a rebellious spirit that could be exploited and that the evil one could and would take advantage of for his own purposes. Ezekiel had high expectations of human conduct before the holiness of God. He wanted his people to live a life pleasing to the Lord. He saw the real possibilities to be gained by repentance. God was and is more than willing to save his people. Have faith and trust in God! God will give Israel a new heart and a new spirit so that they can obey and be faithful to their new Covenant. Ezekiel saw that repentance follows God's initiative to save and he hoped that Israel would come to understand that God, acting in their behalf, is better than shaming themselves by refusing to cooperate with His grace.

The prophet speaks:

Ezekiel was given the responsibility to speak the truth to the people of Israel. He warned them of what was going to happen because they had turned away from the service of the Lord. It did not matter whether the people were willing to listen to the words of the Lord; they must be spoken. One may ask: Where are our leaders today? Where are those individuals willing to speak out on a variety of issues from abortion to worshipping false gods? Where are the hearts of the people? Are we more concerned with offending people than speaking the truth? Are our Church leaders really leading or are they being led? The easy answer is not necessarily the correct answer. Ezekiel was given a mission to be carried out: Speak the truth, trust in God, hope in the future and be accountable to God not to man. Ezekiel states clearly God's intention to deliver his people from their sins and cleanse them from their impurities. The prophets are to remind the people that God will be their God and they will be his people.

Ezekiel

Chapter 1 to 16   **The sovereignty and glory of God**

1:1 – 13	The call of the prophet
1:15 – 25	The vision continues
1:26 – 28	The glory of the Lord
2:1 – 5	Ezekiel's mission
2:6 – 10	Speak my words
3:1 – 4	Eating the scroll
3:5 – 15	Speak to a rebellious house
3:17 – 21	The prophet as watchman
3:22 – 27	Ezekiel's dumbness
4:1 – 8	Symbolic acts of siege and exile
4:9 – 15	Scarcity of food during a siege
5:1 – 4	Shave your head and beard
5:5 – 12	Judgment is coming
5:13 – 15	The wrath of God
6:1 – 7	I will destroy your idols
6:8 – 10	I will spare some of you
6:11 – 14	The sword, starvation and disease
7:1 – 4	The end is near
7:5 – 14	I hold your conduct against you
7:15 – 27	I am the Lord your God
8:1 – 13	Abominations in the temple
8:14 – 18	I will not listen to them
9:1 – 11	Slaughter of the idolaters
10:1 – 11	God's glory leaves Jerusalem
10:12 – 18	God leaves the temple

11:1 – 13	Judgment on the house of Israel
11:14 – 21	A new heart, a new spirit
12:1 – 6	A rebellious house
12:7 – 20	Symbolic acts
12:21 – 28	Prophecy ridiculed
13:1 – 12	Woe to false prophets
13:13 – 16	You will see the fury of God
13:17 – 21	Against witches
14:1 – 11	Say to the house of Israel
14:12 – 20	Noah, Daniel and Job
14:21 – 23	Personal responsibility
15:1 – 8	The parable of the vine
16:1 – 14	The unfaithful spouse
16:15 – 50	Jerusalem the prostitute
16:51 – 58	Samaria and Sodom recalled
16:59 – 63	An everlasting Covenant

Chapters 17 to 24 The Fall of Jerusalem

17:1 – 18	The eagles and the vine
17:19 – 24	He ignored his oath
18:1 – 13	Do the right thing
18:14 – 20	The righteous will live
18:21 – 32	God will judge the house of Israel
19:1 – 9	Allegory of the lions
19:10 – 14	Allegory of the vine and the branch
20:1 – 12	Israel's history of infidelity
20:13 – 17	They rebelled against me
20:18 – 26	Their children rebelled

20:27 – 44	Speak to the house of Israel
21:1 – 10	The sword of the Lord
21:11 – 22	Act symbolic of the city's fall
21:23 – 32	Nebuchadnezzar at the crossroads
21:33 – 37	Against the Ammonites
22:1 – 12	The sins of Jerusalem
22:13 – 26	I will disperse and scatter you
22:27 – 31	Officials and prophets mislead you
23:1 – 34	The two sisters
23:35 – 45	Samaria and Jerusalem
23:46 – 49	You will pay for your idolatry
24:1 – 14	The allegory of the pot
24:15 – 24	A sign to the people
24:25 – 27	The end of Ezekiel's dumbness

Chapters 25 to 32   Judgment on the Nations

25:1-7	Against Ammon
25:8 – 11	Against Moah
25:12 – 14	Against Edom
25:15 – 17	Against the Philistines
26:1 – 13	Against the city of Tyre
26:14 – 21	The destruction of Tyre
27:1 – 36	The shallow glory of Tyre
28:1 – 10	The prince of Tyre
28:11 – 19	A funeral lament for Tyre
28:20 – 24	Against Sidon
28:25 – 26	I will restore the house of Israel
29:1 – 16	Egypt the crocodile

29:17 – 21	The wages of Nebuchadnezzar
30:1 – 19	The day of the Lord approaches
30:20 – 26	Pharaoh's broken arm
31:1 – 14	Allegory of the cypress
31:15 – 18	Egypt's arrogance punished
32:1 – 16	Dirge over pharaoh
32:17 – 32	Dirge over Egypt

Chapters 33 to 39 Salvation for Israel

33:1 – 9	The prophet a watchman
33:10 – 20	Individual retribution
33:21 – 22	The fugitive from Jerusalem
33:23 – 29	The survivors in Judah
33:30 – 33	Popular misunderstanding
34:1 – 13	Parable of the shepherds
34:14 – 21	God will rescue his sheep
34:22 – 31	I will save my flock
35:1 – 15	Against Edom
36:1 – 15	To the mountains of Israel
36:16 – 32	Regeneration of the people
36:33 – 38	I will cleanse of your guilt
37:1 – 14	Vision of the dry bones
37:15 – 22	Two sticks
37:23 – 28	A covenant of peace
38:1 – 23	First prophecy against Gog
38:14 – 16	Second prophecy against Gog
39:1 – 20	Third prophecy against Gog
39:21 – 29	Israel's return

Chapter 40 to 48   The New Israel

40:1 – 5	The man with the measure
40:6 – 16	The east gate
40:17 – 19	The outer gate
40:20 – 23	The north gate
40:24 – 27	The south gate
40:28 – 38	Gates of the inner court
40:39 – 47	Side rooms
40:48 – 49	The temple building
41:1 – 15	The holy of holies
41:16 – 26	The interior of the temple
42:1 – 14	Other structures
42:15 – 20	Measuring the outer court
43:1 – 9	The glory of the Lord returns
43:10 – 12	The law of the temple
43:13 – 27	The altar
44:1 – 3	The closed gate
44:4 – 9	Admission to the temple
44:10 – 14	Levites
44:15 – 31	Priests
45:1 – 8	The sacred tract
45:9 – 12	Weights and measures
45:13 – 17	Offerings
45:18 – 24	The Passover
45:25	The feast of booths
46:1 – 15	Sabbaths and ritual laws
46:16 – 18	The prince and the land
46:19 – 24	The temple kitchens

47:1 – 12	The wonderful stream
47:13 – 20	The New Israel
47:21 – 23	The northern portions
48:1 – 22	The sacred tract
48:23 – 29	The southern portions
48:30 – 35	The gates of the city

The New American Bible: pages 916-960
Copyright: Catholic Publishers, Inc. 1971
A Division of Thomas Nelson, Inc.

CHAPTER THIRTEEN
The Prophet Haggai

Haggai

King Cyrus of Persia had conquered Babylon in 539 B.C. and in 538 had issued a decree that the exiled Israelites could return to their homeland. The first group to return did so by 536. They had begun construction on the destroyed temple. Because of local opposition they soon ceased work on the temple. Nothing was done for sixteen years when the prophet Haggai appeared on the scene. The book of Haggai covers about four months, from August 29 through December 18, 520 B.C. Haggai's message was simple and straightforward: the temple needs to be rebuilt. As one of the first post-exilic prophets, he along with Zechariah took up the cause of rebuilding the temple. The effort of the governor, Zerubbabel and the high priest, Joshua had not gotten beyond the laying of the foundation. The Israelites had been through a great deal. They had suffered the loss of their monarchy, their temple, their homeland, their sense of false security and their belief that no matter how they behaved the Lord would protect them. It was a time of soul-searching and a time of adjustment to a totally new way of life. Now they found themselves returned to their homeland and yet things had not worked in their favor. They were in the midst of a drought and the harvest had been sparse. The wonderful restoration promised by earlier prophets had not occurred. It was in this setting that Haggai exhorted his people to rebuild the temple. His primary focus was aimed at moving the people out of their self-centered complacency and encouraging them to do what had to be done, namely rebuild the temple. The people in Jerusalem had halted construction on the temple. They did however have time to finish their own houses. David had lamented the fact that, while he lived in a palace, God's presence among his people was marked with a tent. It was David's son Solomon who had constructed the first temple. It was up to the people to rebuild what had been destroyed. It was Haggai's responsibility to point out to the people and their leaders that God was not pleased with their behavior once again. The people had used as an excuse for not continuing work on the temple, economic conditions. Haggai tells the people it was the failure to build the temple that had caused the economic difficulties and so the time to build was now. God wants his house in which to dwell. The primacy of God and his house is used as a motive of encouragement to the builders. Work on the temple began only three weeks after Haggai's rebuke. Although the people energetically began to rebuild the temple, the resources of this rag-tag group of returned exiles could not compare with the resources available to Solomon. Thus, their reconstructed temple fell far short of the glory of Solomon's temple. Some of the old timers even wept when they saw the difference. God was pleased with the people's efforts. The temple was a symbol of the community restored to God's favor. Postexilic prophecy begins with Haggai, who received the word of the Lord in 520 B.C. The Jews, who returned from their exile in Babylon, had encountered formidable obstacles in their efforts to re-establish Jewish life in Judah. The Samaritans had succeeded in delaying the rebuilding of the temple; but after Darius acceded to the throne permission was given to resume the work. It was at this critical moment, when defeatism and apathy had overtaken his repatriated countrymen, Haggai came forward with his enthusiasm and his exhortations to encourage the Jews to complete the great task at hand. God had commissioned him to lead the charge, to see to it that the work got finished. Haggai was the right cheerleader, appearing at the right moment in history, to insure success in this endeavor, the completion of the temple. There were objections, namely poor economic conditions, lack of resources and preoccupation with the distractions of life etc. Haggai's answers were direct and to the point, the reason for the present economic conditions was because there was no temple; true it would not be as great as the temple Solomon had constructed and it doesn't matter because God is pleased with it; they had managed to build their own homes while neglecting God's home. Haggai's final comment covered all their objections; stop with the excuses and get the temple built. Haggai's book consists of only two chapters containing four oracles dated between August and December of 520 B.C. His message was simple and straightforward: the temple needs to be rebuilt. The people had halted construction on the temple. God calls the people to task, their priorities were not right. They had been able to finish building their own homes while God's house lay in ruins. The land was suffering from drought and hunger, poverty and crop failure because they neglected the house of God. The prophet calls on the people to strive for holiness in their personal actions. The people must return their hearts to the service of the Lord. Haggai points out that such disregard for honoring God had not resulted in blessing. On the contrary, the people were struggling economically precisely because they were not honoring God. God assures the people that the glory of the new temple will be greater than the glory of the former temple. Looking to the future it is Jesus who brings true glory to the temple. Likewise, the healing of the beggar by Peter and John takes place in the temple. It is here that the Apostles proclaim the new way, the very temple that will be destroyed by the Romans in the year 70 A.D. "I will fill this house with glory..." (Haggai 2:7) The apostle John witnesses these events.

Reflections and Comments

Hear the word of the Lord:

It is not surprising that the people were finally willing to listen to their prophets. They had ignored twelve of the sixteen prophets at their own peril. They had been warned about the Assyrians, the Babylonians, and the Persians. They knew beforehand that their temple would be destroyed and that they would be exiled from their homeland. There is a saying that expresses the reality, "Hindsight is twenty-twenty". The people of Israel knew what was going to happen. The prophets had given amble warning. They finally had to admit that they understood, albeit after the fact. Moses in the Book of Deuteronomy had laid out what would happen should the people adopt the behaviors of their neighbors. It had all become true. The message for us today is to look at what happened to a people who refused to open their eyes and see that what happened to the Israelites could very likely happen to us. Have we not gradually turned away from serving the Lord? Have are leaders not been reluctant to stand up for what is right? Is not the first question out of the mouths of the people, what's in it for me?

Richard C. Kelley and Leo F. Peterson

Haggai

Chapter 1   **A prophetic message**

1:1 – 2   The prophet Haggai is called
1: 3 – 7   Look at what you are doing
1:8 – 11   Rebuild the Lord's temple
1:12 – 15   The leaders respond to the Lord

Chapter 2   **The future glory of the temple**

2:1 – 9   Prayers of encourage
2:10 – 14   The role of the priesthood
2:15 – 19   Build the temple and God will bless
2:20 – 23   I will be your God

The New American Bibles: pages 1028 – 1030
Copyright: Catholic Publishers, Inc. 1971
A Division of Thomas Nelson, Inc.

CHAPTER FOURTEEN

The Prophet
Zechariah

Richard C. Kelley and Leo F. Peterson

Zechariah

Our fourteenth prophet is Zechariah. The postexilic prophets are Haggai, Zechariah and Malachi. The kings and the people of Judah insisted on worshipping foreign idols, violating Moses' call to be faithful to the commandments of the Lord and trusting that their empty practice of temple rituals would keep them in God's good graces, in spite of all the pre-exilic warning to the contrary. The postexilic community is living in an interim period between future restoration and salvation and the beginning of a new community returning to the service of the Lord. Zechariah was a contemporary of Haggai. It appears that like, Ezekiel, Zechariah was a priest. The name Zechariah was held by at least thirty men in the Old Testament. He was a leader in the restoration of the nation of Israel following their captivity and eventual release by the Persian nation. The Book of Zechariah looks beyond the present day task of rebuilding the temple, which he considered important, to the expectation of a promised restoration and salvation. He looks to a time when all the nations will receive the blessings of God. Zechariah begins his testimony by asking the people to return to the service of the Lord. He reminds them that God's word given to the prophets lives forever. Zechariah receives eight night visions. An angel accompanies each vision to explain it to Zechariah. The visions explain the current situation while containing a look at the future. The visions begin with the four horses patrolling the earth reporting to God that the entire world is at rest. The first vision certifies that God will bring about the promised restoration to Israel. The second vision sees four horns representing the powerful nations who destroyed and scattered Israel and Judah. Israel's enemies are many and are all around them. God will rescue Israel from those nations, a theme that the prophets had repeated over the years, and all Israel has to do is return to the service of the Lord. The visions continue demonstrating the power of God to bring about change, to restore and save Israel from the evils of the world. The visions are God's way of declaring that He will take care of a united Israel. He wants Israel to stand up for what is right, show mercy and compassion, protect the widow and orphan, turn to the lord with all their hearts and do what is pleasing in the eyes of God. God promises to come and dwell among His people. The first part of the Book of Zechariah is filled with hope and optimism. God describes a day when the people will gather on the land and will live in peace and prosperity. The second part of the Book of Zechariah focuses on the coming time of restoration and the establishment of God's kingdom. This section contains a large amount of messianic material. The final unit of Zechariah is especially rich with passages that the New Testament will connect to Jesus. The day of God will arrive. The people will be cleansed of their sins. The eyes of all people will be opened and the will of the Lord will be done. When John the Baptist sent his disciples to Jesus, they asked Jesus, "Are you the one who is to come or should we look for another?" Jesus told them; "Go and tell John what you have seen and heard: the blind regain their sight, the lame walk, lepers are cleansed, the deaf hear, the dead are raised, the poor have the good news proclaimed to them." (Luke 7:22) Through the centuries we have seen Israel prosper, fall, prosper, fall and prosper only to fall again. Ignoring and turning away from the service of the Lord leads to hopelessness and anguish. Remember who is in charge! Have faith and know that the Lord will always prevail! The message of the prophet Zechariah is very similar to that of Haggai. He appeared in 520 only a few months after the prophet Haggai. He prophesied for two years longer than Haggai. Zechariah was born in Babylon during the time of the Babylonian captivity. He had returned to Jerusalem with the fifty thousand Jewish exiles. After their return, an altar had been built to renew the burnt sacrifices. In the second year the foundation of the temple was laid. Because of the opposition of the people of the land, work on the temple was halted. The book of Zechariah constituted one of the most compact apocalyptic (i.e. end time) prophetic books of the Old Testament. He calls on the people to repent, "Be not like yours fathers…" Zechariah 1:4. He turns his attention to the future and the visions he received from the Lord. The visions indicated that God would keep His promise and restore Israel. Zechariah offers hope for a brighter future. He knows that God will transform the whole world into a new paradise, representing a new state of thought that will unfold gradually over the centuries to come. Everything is in place. The coming of the Lord is a matter of time. We today await the final chapters of God's salvation plan knowing that, in the end evil will be overcome. Zechariah shares Haggai's concern for the rebuilding of the temple. He sees the day when God will create a cleansed and purified community. He predicts the coming of a new messianic age. The chosen people will be gathered from the ends of the earth and returned to the land promised to Abraham. He makes a special point of emphasizing the role of the high priest Joshua, Zechariah himself being a priest. He uses highly symbolic images, along with visions, to make his point. A new day is coming, a time to be awakened and prepared for the coming of the Lord. Instead of making the message simple, he uses colorful descriptions to mask its true meaning to all except those who know what the prophet is talking about. On the question of fasting God declares that He is more interested in how we treat one another than in man-made rituals. Zechariah focuses his attention upon restoration and the establishment of God's king. A great deal of the book of Zechariah speaks of future events. The passion narratives of the Gospels quote from Zechariah to demonstrate that Jesus is indeed the Messiah. From his humble entrance into Jerusalem, to his betrayal, to the famous quote, "strike the shepherd and the sheep will be scattered". (Mathew 26:31)

Reflections and Comments

Eschatology:

The term "eschatology" from the Greek *eschatos*, (last) was coined in Germany in the early 19th century, when it was used primarily for that branch of theology which dealt with the last things: death, judgment, heaven and hell. It deals not only with the end of history, but also with God's sovereign plan and purposes for creation. Biblical hope rests on God's covenant faithfulness to destroy evil, rescue his people and restore his creation. Throughout history, people have had different views of the future. The Bible and Zechariah gave hope to generations who had lost enthusiasm for a brighter future. The prophets were convinced that God was in charge and all that was needed was trust and faith in Him. The prophets spent most of their time proclaiming the broken covenant and announcing a coming judgment. A smaller but very important part of their message dealt with the future restoration and the coming of a Messiah. The prophets declared that history was moving toward a God-controlled end. They were convinced that good will overcome evil and that God will never abandon His people.

Apocalypse

Webster's New World Dictionary and Thesaurus tells us that the word "apocalypse" means a revelation of a violent struggle in which evil will be destroyed. It was a literary genre that flourished in the period between the Old Testament and the New Testament. It takes its name from the Greek word *"apoalypsis"* meaning "revelation". Visions of heaven and the future, featuring extraordinary creatures and events, focused attention on a whole new world. It is most often identified with the Book of Daniel in the Old Testament and the Book of Revelation in the New Testament. Interestingly enough, prophecy speaks to those who have backslidden and begs them to repent, while apocalypse speaks to the faithful and urges them to persevere. The prophets ask the people to think about what they are doing. Their message was one of repentance 'return to the Lord', 'obey his commandments' and 'trust that things will get better'. Apocalypse recognizes that in the end God will be triumphant. The Lord can be trusted no matter how bad things may look. God's words will never pass away.

Zechariah

Chapter 1 to 6   **A call to repentance**

1:1 – 6	The necessity of conversion
1:7 – 13	The four horsemen
1:14 – 17	I will rebuild my house
2:1 – 4	Four horns and four blacksmiths
2:5 – 9	The man with the measuring cord
2:10 – 17	I will dwell in your midst
3:1 – 7	Joshua the high priest
3:8 – 10	Signs of things to come
4:1 – 5	A lampstand and two olive trees
4:6 – 10	Not by might, not by power
4:11 – 14	The explanation
5:1 – 4	The flying scroll
5:5 – 11	The basket of wickedness
6:1 – 8	The four chariots
6:9 – 15	The coronation

Chapters 7 to 8   **Ritual and restoration**

7:1 – 7	True fasting
7:8 – 14	The word came to Zechariah
8:1 – 13	Judah and Zion restored
8:14 – 18	Speak the truth to one another
8:19 – 23	Festivals for the house of Judah

Chapters 9 to 14

9:1 – 8	Judgment of the nations
9:9 – 10	The king's entrance into Jerusalem
9:11 – 17	Restoration of the people
10:1 – 12	The new order of things
11:1 – 3	The fall of pagan tyrants
11:4 – 17	The allegory of the shepherds
12:1 – 9	Jerusalem, God's instrument
12:10 – 14	The fate of Jerusalem's foes
13:1 – 6	The end of falsehood
13:7 – 9	The song of the sword
14:1 – 5	The fight for Jerusalem
14:6 – 11	Jerusalem restored
14:12 – 15	The day of the Lord
14:16 – 21	The future

The New American Bible: pages 1031 – 1039
Copyright: Catholic Publishers, Inc. 1971
A Division of Thomas Nelson, Inc.

CHAPTER FIFTEEN

The Prophet
Joel

Joel

Our fifteenth prophet is Joel. His book contains no historical reference tying his prophecy to a specific time in history. The prophet Joel is not mentioned anywhere else in the Old Testament outside his book. Most scholars feel it was written just before the Assyrian invasion or just before the Babylonian invasion. The latter view seems to have the strongest support. It is this view that our study holds. Joel is believed to be a temple prophet. He prophesied in Judah at the temple in Jerusalem around the year 500. Much of what the prophets proclaimed comes directly from Deuteronomy 28. Joel's message focuses upon his vivid description of a locust plague. Plagues of locusts moving across the land were a recurring and terrifying phenomenon. Locust swarms can cover up to 400 square miles. Each square mile could contain 100 million insects each of which could consume its own weight each day. Joel's description of a locust plague and an invading army was obvious to his listeners, and he was not the only prophet to make that comparison. The people recognized just how devastating a locust plague could be. Joel's point would not be lost on the people who had experienced this phenomenon. Moses' description found in Deuteronomy 28:49 foretells just how completely an invading army, raised up by the hand of God, was capable of destroying everything in its path. Like the locust, nothing is left; no grain, no livestock, indeed nothing remains. All the people have to do to avoid such devastation is trust in the Lord, obey the commandments and put God first in one's life. Joel reminds his people that God is slow to anger and willing to forgive if the people will only repent. Joel's words contain a delicate balance between judgment and restoration a call to repentance coupled with the potential of great reward for doing the right thing. One of the more prominent themes found in Joel is the day of God. Of the many passages found in the Old Testament, Amos 5:18 and Isaiah 13:6 come to mind, along with Jeremiah 46:10, Ezekiel 7:10, Zephaniah 1:7 and Zechariah 14:1 as noted. Joel 2:1 – 2, "…the day of God is coming … a day of clouds and thick darkness." Before it the earth quakes, the heavens tremble. Sun and moon are darkened and the stars lose their brightness. This day is a day of distress, of darkness and gloom, a day of trumpet-blast and battle cry. Men will be overcome with fear; in their panic they go about as blind men unable to save themselves, and the earth is to be consumed with the fire of God's zealous wrath. The day of God is not one that is looked forward to with expectant anticipation. The day of God is associated with Our Lord's second coming, a time when all will be judged. Luke 21:26 "People will die of fright in anticipation of what is coming upon the world…" Those who are faithful, who obey the commandments and trust in God, will be spared. If people will only change their hearts and return to the Lord, the day of doom will become a day of blessing for them. There is no more paradoxical book of the Bible than Joel. Pervading this ever changing sequence of events is the tremendous energy contained in the imagery from start to finish, with everything centered on Joel's description of a plague of locust. The strength of the Book of Joel lies in its confident hope that God will never forget his people or refuse to hear their prayers. The lesson for today is never cease praying. Jesus told his followers to pray at all times. Joel knows that the final struggle between the forces of good and the forces of evil will result in God establishing His sovereignty. The outcome is certain. The time is unknown. Do what is right, have faith in the Lord and know that good things will happen. The book is characterized by movement from specific concern with the plague of locusts to a more general prophecy of universal judgment. It is reasonable to suggest that the book of Joel is one of the later prophetic books with a date after 500. He prophesied in Judah, in Jerusalem and in the temple. He uses an agricultural crisis, a locust plague, to warn the people of a worse disaster if they ignore his preaching. He urges them to appreciate just how important their faithfulness is, that it will lead to a brighter future. If the people do penance, God will call a halt to the plague and restore prosperity. God promises to send his holy spirit upon the people. When the world is in trouble it typically returns to the temple pleading for God's help. Following a tragedy people return to their church-going ways. It is no different today. It is a way of showing their need for help and a means for expressing their hope that God would bring some relief to a people who are hurting. In urging the people to use a crisis as an occasion for reform, the prophet is bringing some good out of a bad situation. The prophetic idea of salvation is primarily concerned with the welfare of the people. Joel recognizes that putting God first in life is of utmost importance if survival and salvation are to be achieved. The Book of Joel consists of two speeches. The first has to do with a warning of judgment that is sure to come for failing to appreciate all that God has done for his people. The second is expressed in the optimism that Joel feels is to be found in the hope for a bright future, based on the belief that the people will return to the service of the Lord. The traditional prophetic approach was to use a crisis as an occasion for repentance and reform. By this means, the prophets hope to bring some good out of a bad situation. Churches tend to be full when disaster strikes. Theologically the message is one of hope built on experience. The devastation visited upon Israel was immense. However, if God responded to Israel's cry for help, for Joel it was at the very least a sign that God would not abandon his people. God was still in their midst. Armed with that conviction, there was every reason to hope that the reversal of fortune would continue and bring a final vindication in Israel's favor. As has been indicated, Joel's optimism rested upon the firm belief that once Israel returned to the service of the Lord, all things would be resolved. The theme of the book of Joel centers upon the "Day of the Lord", an expression found in the Old Testament. It refers to any period of time in which God deals directly with the human situation, either in judgment or in mercy. God desires to save all mankind. All He asks in return is faithfulness and service to the Lord.

Reflections and Comments

The promise of the Holy Spirit:

In addition to material blessings, the prophets promised that God would pour out His Spirit in the day of the Lord. At the beginning of chapter three in the book of Joel we read, "Then afterward I will pour out my Spirit upon all mankind." (3:1) The Holy Spirit is active in the world today. Granted the world tends not to listen to or to hear what the Spirit has to say, but that does not mean He is not working. His reception does not determine whether He acts. God's grace is all around us. Open your hearts to the Lord! Listen to what He has to say! He cannot help you if you refuse to listen. In the Old Testament the spirit is referred to as the wind. It is the breath of God; it is a sensible manifestation of the Divine Presence and power. It is communicated to living beings but it never becomes a part of the structure of the living being. The Spirit is said to clothe; to be poured out and leaped upon. One may be filled with the Holy Spirit. It can never be controlled by the person. It is free to come and go. The breath of God is frequently represented as the principle of life for all living beings. Life is sacred, a fact that the modern world appears to have forgotten.

The Holy Spirit:

There are many Old Testament images of the spirit of God. Biblical images of the Spirit emphasize sensible things known best by experiencing them. The force of the wind, the intimacy of breathing, the dove, fire and the oil of healing to suggest but a few. At Pentecost the Spirit enters the room with wind and tongues of fire. The apostles were understood in many languages and they appeared filled with the Holy Spirit. The power of the Spirit is beyond all human ability or comprehension. The prophet Joel saw the Spirit descending upon the people of Israel. The early Church recognized the presence of the Holy Spirit as proof and validation that what they were doing, God found pleasing. In today's world the Holy Spirit must indeed be disappointed. People have failed to listen, failed to be receptive, failed to speak the truth and failed to take advantage of all that the Spirit has to offer. Hope and optimism have not yet turned to despair and discouragement, but it appears to be headed there. The words of an enthusiastic Joel have much to offer our world if we would open our hearts to but hear what he has to say. We must have faith and courage in the face of opposition. We must set a good example and as Saint John tells us we must love one another.

Joel

Chapter 1   **Unprecedented disaster**

    1:1 – 4   An agricultural crisis

    1:4 – 10   A wake up call

    1:11 – 12   Look at what has happened

    1:13 – 14   A call to penance

    1:15 – 20   Near is the day of the Lord

Chapter 2   **The day of the Lord**

    2:1 – 10   An attack is coming

    2:11 – 17   Return to the Lord

    2:18 – 20   Prosperity will return

    2:21 – 27   Fear not

Chapter 3   **The final judgment**

    3:1 – 5   I will send my spirit upon the people

Chapter 4   **Judgment upon the nations**

    4:1 – 3   The Lord's time has come

    4:4   8   Vengeance is mine

    4:9 – 12   Listen to the Lord

    4:13 – 16   The valley of decision

| 4:17 | Know that I am the Lord |
| 4:18 – 21 | Salvation for God's elect |

The New America Bible: pages 992-995
Copyright: Catholic Publishers, Inc. 1971
A Division of Thomas Nelson, Inc.

CHAPTER SIXTEEN

The Prophet
Malachi

Malachi

The book of Malachi is generally recognized as the last of the Old Testament "writing prophets". The prophet Malachi was a contemporary of Haggai and Zechariah. His candor regarding the many abuses of the priests and the people of Israel at a time of social decadence and spiritual decline rivaled that of Isaiah. His message of God's love for Israel recalling the miraculous events of the past was aimed at rekindling the enthusiasm and the love relationship God had with His people. Central to Malachi's message is the issue of proper worship. He takes the priests to task for offering faulty sacrifices, blind and lame animals and defective offerings which dishonor the God of Israel. Malachi finds it next to impossible to explain Israel's failure to respond positively to God's love. He addresses the corruption found in the lack of commitment on the part of the priests. Foreign nations have more respect for the God of Israel than the very people who have a personal relationship and who should know better. Malachi points out that their leaders offered unacceptable sacrifices, they supported corrupt priests, they failed to tithe, they divorced and married foreigners, they turned a blind eye to social injustice and refused to honor their covenant relationship. They needed to stop asking: "What's in it for me?" Malachi encountered the same sins that had been experienced by earlier prophets. Even after all that the people had gone through they still persisted in their hardness of heart. Every prophet looked forward to the day when the people would return to the service of the

Lord. The book of Malachi set the stage for one crying in the wilderness. The coming of John the Baptist anticipated in Malachi 3:1 "Lo, I am sending my messenger to prepare the way before me;" preceded the appearance of Jesus the Messiah who was to come. Several centuries were to elapse between the ministry of Malachi and the coming of John the Baptist. There were a number of issues addressed by Malachi. He was unhappy with the lack of appreciative love for the God who had done so much for the people of Israel. He found it difficult to accept the disrespect and dishonor given to the God of Israel. He dealt with the question of the personal guilt associated with the breaking of the covenant relationship. He could not see how the questioning of God's justice and the showing of envy for the prosperity of the wicked was a healthy thing for the people of Israel. He discussed the disobedience to God and the social injustice present therein. Moses had warned the people not to marry pagans as unfaithfulness and remarriage with unbelievers was something detrimental to the purity of the faith. The most troubling issue for Malachi was their attitude, their ignorance, their arrogance, their lack of trust and their unfaithfulness. Malachi's final words "obey Moses and wait for Elijah" bring the study of the prophets to a close. So the Old Testament which began with the statement "In the beginning," ends with the promise of "one who is to come." The Book of Malachi is the last book of the Old Testament. It is post-exile and is dated from 450 to 400, although it contains no historical reference per se. Malachi condemns many of the abuses found in Israel including the laxity of their morals, corruption and lack of devotion on the part of priests. The people are easygoing and weak in the practice of their faith. They are marrying pagans, taking divorce lightly, and failing to pay tithes and offerings which they owe to God. They do not take care of widows, orphans and the poor. Malachi uses the rhetorical question and answer style, similar to a child's catechism. One of the main points that the book of Malachi makes is that God still loves his people and thus will move toward their ultimate restoration. God's love is met with skepticism. The people question how God has shown his love. They have recently returned from exile and they are presently living under Persian rule. The future does not look all that bright. Malachi reminded them just how far short their commitment to God had fallen from the beginning of the covenant relationship. God's plan of restoration is just beginning. It is God's great love that brought them back from exile and his great love that will bring about the future promised blessings and restoration. They must be patient, love God, keep the faith and trust in the Lord. Malachi loves the temple. It is a concrete symbol of God's presence among his people. Malachi stands in a long line of prophets, beginning with Amos, who were critical of the priesthood. In this case, the charge is that the priests have been offering cheap sacrifices and disposing of sick and lame animals instead of offering the healthy and the best ones. No one would think of offering a sick animal to their governor, yet the priests are making such offerings to God. Doing this reflects an attitude of disrespect at the very least and neglect of duty at the most. Malachi's final words bring the prophets to a close. In the Christian canon this book brings the Old Testament to a close. Malachi tells the postexilic community to wait with expectation for the appearance of Elijah, who will signal the great day of God. In the meantime, as they wait, they are to remain obedient to the laws given to Moses. In the New Testament Jesus clearly identifies John the Baptist as a fulfillment of the "messenger" prophecy of Malachi (3:1). When John the Baptist first begins his ministry the connection between him and Malachi is obvious enough that people ask John directly if he is Elijah (John 1:21). Moses and Elijah appear at the transfiguration event (Matthew 17:1 – 13; Mark 9:2 – 13; Luke 9:28 – 36). The book of Malachi ends with a high expectation of what is to come.

Reflections and Comments

The end of our study:

Our journey began with Jonah, the reluctant prophet and was followed by Amos, a sheepherder and dresser of sycamores. Hosea, the prophet with the unfaithful wife, was next. Isaiah, the first of the major prophets considered by some the greatest of the Old Testament prophets was followed by Micah. It was Micah who foretold the birth place of Jesus. Nahum foretold the destruction of Nineveh and was number six in our study. Zephaniah preceded Jeremiah who witness the destruction of Jerusalem. Daniel, the third of the major prophets, with his apocalyptic writing style followed Habakkuk, who question the ways of God. Obadiah wrote the shortest book of the Old Testament and was number eleven on our list. Ezekiel, the fourth of the major prophets, preceded Haggai, the first of the post-exilic prophets. Zechariah, Joel and Malachi rounded out our study. Each prophet contributed their unique prospective to the words God had given them. The people of Israel were in trouble. They had broken the Covenant. They failed to repent of their behavior and were headed for punishment. They were guilty of idolatry, social injustice and religious hypocrisy. Not unlike our society today.

Malachi

Chapter 1	**God's love for Israel affirmed**
1:1 – 5	Israel's failure to respond to God's love
1: 6 – 10	Faulty sacrifices and corrupt priests
1:11 – 14	The people's disrespect highlighted
Chapter 2	**Break not the Covenant**
2:1 – 9	Give the honor due my name
2:10 – 15	The sins of the people
2:16	I hate divorce
2:17	You have wearied the Lord
Chapter 3	**The Lord is coming**
3:1 – 5	The messenger of the covenant
3:6 – 12	Return to me and I will return to you
3:13 – 16	Serve the Lord in all things
3:17 – 21	I will be your God
3:22 – 24	Moses and Elijah

The New American Bible: pages 1040 – 1043
Copyright: Catholic Publishers, Inc. 1971
A Division of Thomas Nelson, Inc.

The Kings of Northern Israel and of Judah (922-586)

Northern Israel		Judah	
Jeroboam I	922-911	Rehoboam	922-915
Nadab	911-910	Abijam	915-913
Baasha	910-887	Asa	913-873
Elah	887-886	Jehoshaphat	873-849
Zimri	886	Jehoram	849-842
Omri	886-875	Ahaziah	842
Ahab	875-854	(Athaliah)	842-837
Ahaziah	854-853	Joash (=Jehoash)	836-797
Jehoram (=Joram)	853-842	Amaziah	797-769
Jehu	842-815	Uzziah (=Azariah)	769-741
Jehoahaz (=Jehoahas)	815-799	Jotham-Ahaz coregency	741-726
Jehoash (Joash)	799-784	Hezekiah	726-697
Jeroboam II	784-744	Manasseh	697-642
Zechariah	744	Amon	640
Shallum	744	Josiah	640-609
Menahem	744-735	Jehoahaz	609
Pekahiah	735-734	Jehoiakim	609-598
Pekah	734-731	Jehoiachin	598
Hoshea	731-722	Zedekiah	598-587

Fall of Samaria	722	Fall of Jerusalem	586
		Babylonian Rule	586-539
		Persian Rule	539-532
		Edict of Cyrus	538

Significant Events in History

1. Samaria destroyed by Assyria in 722 B.C.

2. Jerusalem besieged by Sennacherib in 701 B.C.

3. Thebes was destroyed by the Assyrians in 663 B.C. (High point of Assyrian power)

4. Nineveh destroyed by the Babylonians in 612 B.C.

5. Jerusalem destroyed by the Babylonians in 587 B.C. (The Temple included)

REFERENCES

1. <u>The New Jerome Biblical Commentary</u>

   Edited by: Raymond E. Brown S. S.
                 Joseph A. Fitzmyer S. J.
                 Roland E. Murphy O. Carm.
   Imprimatur: Reverend William J. Kane
                 Vicar General for the Archdiocese
                 of Washington November 15th, 1988
   Publisher: Prentice-Hall, Inc. 1990, 1988
                 A Paramount Communications
                 Company
                 United States of America

2. <u>The New American Bible</u>

   Editors: Members of the Catholic Biblical
                 Association of America
   Imprimatur: Patrick Cardinal O' Boyle, D.D.
                 July 27th, 1970
   Publishers: Catholic Publishers, Inc. 1971
                 Thomas Nelson Publishers
                 Nashville

3. <u>The Catholic Study Bible</u> (Second Edition)

Editors: Donald Senior
                John J. Collins
                Mary Ann Getty
Imprimatur: Reverend John F. Canary S.T. L., D.
                Min.
                Vicar General Archdiocese of
                Chicago
                September 14th, 2005
Publisher: Oxford University Press, Inc. 1990,
                2006, 2011
                198 Madison Avenue, New York.
                New York 10016

4. <u>A Guide To The Bible</u>

Author: Antonio Fuentes
Imprimatur: Joseph A. Carroll
                Diocesan Administrator
                August 25th, 1987
Publisher: Four Courts Press
                7 Malpas Street, Dublin 8

5. <u>Reading The Old Testament An Introduction</u>

Author: Lawrence Boadt
Publisher: Paulist Press
                New York, New York

Copyright: 1984
              The Missionary Society

6. <u>Prophecy And The Prophets</u> in Ancient Israel

    Author: Theodore H. Robinson
    Publisher: Gerald Duckworth & Co. LTD.
                  3, Henrietta Street, London
    Copyright: 1953
                  Riverside Press

7. <u>The Prophets</u>

    Author: Abraham J. Heschel
    Publisher: Harper Perennial & Modern Classics
                  New York, New York
    Copyright: 1962
                  Harper& Row

8. <u>The Message Of The Prophets</u> A Survey of the
    Prophetic and Apocalyptic of the Old Testament

    Author: J. Daniel Hays
    General   Tremper Longman III
    Editor:
    Publisher: Zondervan
                      Grand Rapids, Michigan
    Copyright: 2010
                      Hays

9. <u>The Time Chart of Biblical History</u>

Publisher: Chartwell Books, Inc.
                   A Division of Book Sales, Inc.
Copyright: 2002
                   Third Millennium Trust
                   Chippenham, England

10. <u>Archaeological Commentary On The Bible</u> From Genesis to Revelation…

Author: Gonzalo Baez-Camargo
Publisher: A Doubleday-Galilee Book
                   Doubleday & Company, Inc.
Copyright: 1986
                   Garden City, New York

11. <u>Who Was Who in the Bible</u> The Ultimate A to Z Resource

Publisher: MJF Books
                   Fine Communications
Copyright: 1999
                   By Thomas Nelson Publishers
                   New York, New York

12. <u>An Introduction to the Old Testament Prophetic Books</u>

     Publisher: Moody Publishers
     Copyright: 2007
                   By C. Hassell Bullock
                   Chicago, Illinois

13. <u>The Bible and the Liturgy</u>

     Publisher: University of Notre Dame
     Copyright: 1956
                   By the University of Notre Dame Press
                   Notre Dame, Indiana

14. <u>Pictures by Sharon Vaupel</u>

15. <u>Contributing Editors;</u>
Richard C. Kelley and Leo Peterson

Printed in the United States
By Bookmasters